THE OUTRAGE PARADOX

THE OUTRAGE PARADOX

The Cult of Moral Superiority and Rise of Manufactured Victimhood

ROBERT T. YARBOROUGH

Andborough Publishing

Publisher's Cataloging-in-Publication Data
Yarborough, Robert T., 1960–
The Outrage Paradox: The Cult of Moral Superiority and Rise of Manufactured Victimhood / Robert T. Yarborough.
— First edition.
p. cm.
Includes bibliographical references.

ISBN: 979-8-9912582-5-8
    1. Outrage—Psychological aspects. 2. Emotional resilience. 3. Social media—Psychological effects. 4. Cultural criticism. 5. Addiction—Social aspects. 6. Emotional detachment—Self-help. I. Title.
BF575.O88 Y37 2025
158.1 — dc23
LCCN: 2025911985

Printed in the United States of America
10 9 8 7 6 5 4 3 2 1

Dedication

To my three incredibly strong-minded children.

Never forget the strength of quiet conviction, the power of genuine thought, and the freedom found in thinking for yourselves.

Shape your future with reason, resilience, a fierce commitment to authenticity, clarity over noise, truth over comfort, and courage over convenience.

We'd Love to Hear From You!

Thank you so much for reading this book-it means the world to me. If you found it helpful, inspiring, or just enjoyable, would you take a moment to leave a review? Your feedback not only helps others but also keeps me motivated to create more valuable content for you.

Here's how you can leave a review:

1. Scan the QR code on this page to go directly to the author's page.

2. Or, visit your Amazon Orders page, find this book, and click "Write a Product Review."

**Your kind words make a big difference.
Thank you for your support!**

Table of Contents

Chapter Two

Chapter Three

Chapter Five

Chapter Eight

Chapter Nine

Chapter Twelve

Epilogue

Appendix A

Author Preface

"People will do anything, no matter how absurd, in order to avoid facing their own souls."

— Carl Jung

Outrage feels good. It's intoxicating, immediate, and—if we're honest with ourselves—deeply satisfying. It offers the illusion of clarity in a world that's anything but clear. It tells us we're right, that we're on the right side of history, and that anyone who dares to disagree is not just mistaken but morally deficient. In those moments, outrage doesn't whisper—it roars.

We've all felt it. I've felt it too.

But somewhere along the way, outrage stopped being a fleeting emotional response and became something else entirely—an addiction. We refresh newsfeeds, scroll through comment sections, and engage in endless online battles, not because it leads to any meaningful change but because the outrage itself has become the reward. The dopamine hit that comes with every angry post, every indignant share, keeps us coming back for more.

This book was born from a simple but unsettling realization: we're not just reacting to a chaotic world—we're being conditioned to stay outraged. And the cost? Our mental health, relationships, intellectual freedom, and, ultimately, our humanity.

The Outrage Paradox isn't a manifesto against caring—it's an exploration of why the modern obsession with being offended is not about empathy or justice. It's about power, ego, and the deeply human—but often destructive—need to be right. Worse still, it's about how that need is being manipulated by those who profit from our perpetual outrage.

This book isn't comfortable. It challenges assumptions, especially the ones that feel safest to hold. But it's not about preaching or telling you how to think. It's about inviting you to pause, to reflect, and to ask: Is my outrage serving me—or am I serving it?

What follows is not just an analysis of how we got here but a roadmap for how to break free. Because here's the hard truth: real empowerment doesn't come from shouting the loudest or being the most offended. It comes from reclaiming your peace, your clarity, and—above all—your freedom from the outrage machine.

This is not a call to apathy. It's a call to sovereignty.

With gratitude…

—Robert T. Yarborough
May 2025

Introduction

"Whoever is out of patience is out of possession of their soul."

— Francis Bacon

There is a tension you can feel but cannot quite name. It lives in your gut when you open the news, in your chest when you scroll through comments, in the tightness behind your eyes after too much time online. It's a tension that doesn't come from violence or catastrophe, but from the constant emotional static of being outraged. Again. And again.

We live in a time when offense is no longer the exception, it is the expectation.

Outrage has become the language of belonging. To prove you care, you must perform your indignation. To remain accepted, you must show allegiance to the right causes, the right phrases, the right emotional cues. Subtlety is suspect. Nuance is betrayal. Silence is violence. And even agreement, if it lacks enthusiasm, can be grounds for suspicion.

This is not a new phenomenon. Human history is littered with moral panics and ideological purges. But something about this moment feels different. Because now, outrage isn't just a social dynamic, it's a currency. It is monetized, weaponized, and incentivized. It is algorithmically promoted, politically exploited, and emotionally addictive. What was once an occasional flare of moral concern has become a way of life.

But here's the question few dare to ask: Is all this outrage actually helping?

Are we becoming a more just society, or just a more reactive one? Are we solving problems, or simply intensifying them with louder words and shorter tempers? Are we defending others, or just protecting our egos under the banner of righteousness?

This book is not an argument against caring. It is not a defense of apathy. And it is certainly not an endorsement of cruelty or indifference.

What it is is a guide for those who feel like something has gone wrong—who sense that behind all the noise, something essential is being lost: our capacity to think clearly, to feel compassion deeply, and to act with integrity instead of impulse.

Each chapter will explore a different dimension of outrage culture—not to condemn those caught in its grip, but to illuminate how we got here, what it's costing us, and how we might begin to step out of the cycle.

You will not find easy villains in these pages. There are no caricatures, no strawmen to burn. Only questions to sit with, systems to examine, and habits to notice.

Because healing begins not with accusation, but with awareness.

And freedom is not when we shout louder than the crowd, but when we stop needing to shout at all.

Welcome to a quieter conversation.

One that invites clarity over noise, compassion over performance, and presence over panic.

Let's begin.

Chapter One

The Nature of Offense: How Private Discomfort Became Public Spectacle

We can always choose to perceive things differently. We can focus on what's wrong in our life, or we can focus on what's right.

— Marianne Williamson

The Modern Landscape of Offense

Think about the last time you were offended. Did you pause and reflect, or did you feel the urge to announce it? In today's world, offense has become less about personal reflection and more about public declaration. It is no longer enough to feel hurt—one must be seen as hurt. And in this transformation, the true meaning of offense has been lost. Offense is no longer just a feeling—it's a currency. In the marketplace of outrage, the more publicly you display your grievance, the more social capital you gain. And like any currency, the more it is printed and spent, the less value it holds..

The sensation of being offended is a natural human response—a signal that our personal boundaries have been crossed. Yet, in our current culture, that private signal has been amplified and weaponized, evolving into a spectacle that is broadcast for all to see. The shift from internal grievance to external performance is one of the most profound yet under appreciated changes in our society today.

> *It is no longer enough to feel hurt—one must be seen as hurt. In today's culture, offense is not just a reaction—it's a performance.*

No longer is it sufficient to simply feel hurt; one must also display that hurt, often with elaborate fanfare. Social media has acted as a great catalyst in this transformation, carrying what was once a quiet, personal experience into a public arena where each "like," supportive comment, or digital nod of approval further fuels the spectacle. In this way, personal outrage is converted into social capital.

The cultural fixation with being offended has, paradoxically, become a marker of moral significance. In an age where status is increasingly measured by the ability to claim virtuous suffering, offense itself is elevated to a form of currency. To appear continuously aggrieved is often taken as evidence of moral clarity. Yet, in truth, this is rarely about genuine harm. The modern landscape of offense seldom concerns itself with true injury or legitimate grievance. Instead, it serves as a tool—a means by which individuals assert dominance, claim moral authority, and exert influence over others. The display of hurt becomes a way to control discourse, to silence dissent, and to assert ideological supremacy.

This phenomenon is not accidental. Digital platforms, which thrive on emotional engagement and moral fervor, have nurtured and amplified it. Every tweet, headline, and viral video is designed not to resolve conflict but to provoke reaction. In this economy of unending indignation, offense is not simply a response—it is a strategy.

The true question is not whether offense has a place in modern discourse, but rather: What transpires when being offended becomes more about asserting power than upholding principle?

Perhaps even more gently, we must ask: How much of our own outrage reflects an inner truth, and how much is merely a performance dictated by external pressures? When offense becomes a currency, one must consider the cost—what does it reveal about our true nature when our greatest strength lies not in creation, compassion, or mindful thought but simply in our ability to feel and display offense?

What Does It Mean to Be Offended?

To truly understand the cultural spectacle that offense has become, we must return to its origins—its traditional meaning, unadorned by modern embellishment. To be offended is to experience an inner emotional signal—a subtle flare that something in our space has been disturbed, that a boundary has been crossed, whether that boundary is moral, social, or deeply personal.

Historically, offense was a deeply subjective experience, one rooted in personal dignity and the prevailing societal norms of its time. It was not about public display but about a quiet, internal discomfort—a alert from within that a slight or injustice had been encountered. This inner reaction often arose from a sense of moral injury or disrespect—a feeling that one's very sense of being had been diminished. Philosophers like John Stuart Mill recognized this complexity, suggesting that while individuals should be free to express themselves, society also bears the responsibility to honor the delicate balance between free expression and personal dignity.[1]

> *When everything is offensive, nothing is. The inflation of outrage has made true injustice harder to see.*

At its highest expression, offense serves as a protective mechanism—an inner boundary that shields us from genuine harm. It is the body's and mind's way of signaling that our core values or our sense of self are under threat. For example, when one experiences a racist insult, the resulting offense is not only understandable, it is a natural response—a quiet, protective alert that one's dignity or human worth has been challenged. In such moments, offense is not a performance; it is an honest, instinctive call for respect and fairness.

Yet, over time, this natural and protective instinct has grown blurred within a culture that often elevates personal discomfort to the level of deep moral transgression. Once, harm meant something tangible—a wound, an attack, a real violation. But today, harm is whatever we declare it to be. Disagreement is 'violence.' Words are 'assault.' The term 'trauma' is now applied as freely to an uncomfortable conversation as it once was to life-threatening events. This is what psychologists call 'concept creep'—when the definition of harm expands so far that

---

[1] (On Liberty, 1859)

everything becomes offensive, and nothing is taken seriously.[2] As a result, even minor disagreements or the simple encounter with an opposing view may be experienced as a personal affront.

This merging of genuine harm with subjective discomfort is more than just a shift in language—it carries real consequences. It diminishes the profound nature of true injustice by equating trivial offenses with actual violations of dignity. When the simple discomfort of encountering a differing opinion is treated as if it were a deep, personal injury, the space for open, heartfelt dialogue narrows. We find ourselves in a society that grows ever more sensitive, yet paradoxically less compassionate, as the true suffering becomes diluted amidst a sea of manufactured grievances.

Let it be clear: Not every instance of offense is unwarranted. However, when every disagreement is cast as an act of violence, and every hurt feeling is seen as an attack on one's identity, the vital distinction between real harm and mere discomfort begins to dissolve. And when that distinction disappears, the foundation for meaningful dialogue and true intellectual freedom also begins to crumble.

Self-Reflection: What does it truly mean for you when you feel offended? How might you discern the quiet signal of genuine harm from the transient stirrings of mere discomfort?

Psychological Drivers Behind Being Offended

Before the whirlwind of outrage takes hold, it begins with simpler, more elemental psychological impulses—instincts that, in earlier times, were closely linked to survival, self-preservation, and the fabric of social cohesion. Today, these same inner impulses have been subtly transformed, often serving not the well-being of the individual or the community but rather fueling the ceaseless machinery of modern outrage.

There are three primary inner drivers that prompt us to feel offended: the delicate preservation of the ego, the deep human need for belonging, and the quiet longing for emotional validation. These forces, in their purest form, are natural and spontaneous responses. Yet, in our modern landscape, they have been co-opted by external systems that amplify our emotional reactions rather than soothe them.

---

[2] Haidt & Lukianoff, *The Coddling of the American Mind*, 2018

The Ego's Fragile Fortress

At the core of many instances of offense lies the delicate structure of the ego—a fragile construct that seeks to protect our sense of self. The ego's purpose is to guard our personal identity and maintain a feeling of wholeness in the face of challenges. When our deeply held beliefs are questioned, it is not merely a moment of discomfort; it can feel as if the very essence of our being is under threat. In such moments, being offended becomes a natural, albeit reactive, way to defend our inner self against the discomfort of cognitive dissonance.

In our present social context, this vulnerability of the ego is often heightened by rigid ideologies. The quest to be "right" shifts from a reasoned dialogue into an assertion of moral supremacy—a quiet proclamation that our inner truth stands unchallenged. Public expressions of offense, then, become an implicit gesture of both personal hurt and elevated moral identity—a subtle way of affirming that we belong to the "right" side of our own inner narrative.

Self-Reflection: When your beliefs have been questioned, did you sense a deep, inner disturbance? Was it a call to defend your inner truth or a moment that invited you to simply remain curious?

When the call for virtue grows too loud, the gentle strength of genuine conviction may be lost.

Tribalism and the Need for Belonging

As inherently social beings, our need to belong is woven into the very fabric of our existence. Long ago, being part of a group was essential for survival, offering protection and shared purpose. Today, that innate need persists, albeit in quieter, more internal ways. In the digital age, feelings of offense often become a way to affirm our belonging to a particular community—a reminder of where we feel safe.

Expressing hurt or indignation can serve as an unspoken signal of loyalty to our chosen tribe. In these moments, our inner desire for connection nudges us to align with others who share our sentiments. Digital platforms, with their echoing chambers, make this alignment even more palpable, as shared expressions of grievance further solidify our sense of group identity. It is here that we see a soft yet pervasive distinction between "us" and "them," a quiet reaffirmation of where we belong.

Consider for a moment: To what extent does your sense of belonging shape the way you experience offense? When you express your inner pain, is it a reflection of your personal truth, or does it also affirm your place within a community?

Validation as a Social Reward

Beyond the safeguarding of the ego and the need to belong, there is the quiet pursuit of emotional validation—a yearning to be seen and acknowledged. In our deeply connected world, this inner need for recognition is magnified, inviting us to share our inner experiences with others. Yet, when the quest for validation becomes the primary reason for our expressions of hurt, what began as an internal signal may slowly transform into a public performance.

In moments when we seek external approval, our inner experience of offense shifts from a private alert into a shared display. Each time we express our inner disquiet and receive a nod of approval—a like, a comment, a quiet retweet—we may find that the subtle warmth of recognition encourages us to repeat this act. Over time, this natural cycle can become a pattern where our inner need for authenticity is overshadowed by a soft yet persistent craving for external validation.

Self-Reflection: Have there been times when you shared your inner feelings primarily to receive a sense of connection or approval? Was this act a true reflection of your inner truth or a quiet performance shaped by the desire for recognition?

The craving for external affirmation can become as compelling as any habit, drawing us away from the stillness of true being.

This section reveals that the urge to feel offended arises from very natural and ancient aspects of our human nature. When we become aware of these inner drivers—the fragile fortress of the ego, our intrinsic need for belonging, and the soft pull of external validation—we are offered the opportunity to step back and reconnect with our inner stillness. In doing so, we may find that our reactions, when observed with mindful presence, transform from impulsive responses into chances for deeper understanding and genuine connection.

The Historical Evolution of Offense

Offense, as we understand it today, is not a static idea—it has evolved alongside the shifting values and technologies of society. What was once an intensely personal experience, deeply rooted in honor and dignity, has gradually transformed into a public spectacle—a phenomenon often used to influence and control.

Honor Cultures: When Offense Was Personal

In societies guided by the code of honor, offense was a matter of personal dignity, a quiet signal that one's inner integrity had been challenged. In 17th-century Europe, for example, duels were not mere displays of vanity; they were solemn acts—social contracts in which personal respect was at stake. Consider the infamous duel between Alexander Hamilton and Aaron Burr, a confrontation that went far beyond mere disagreement, emerging instead as a means to restore personal honor. In those times, to be offended carried deep significance; it demanded sincere action, not a performance for an audience.

Yet, not every culture responded with violence. Many societies embraced formal apologies or mediated reconciliations, preserving social harmony without spectacle. In those moments, the feeling of offense was a private call to restore balance—a response that was intimate and free from public display, unamplified by the modern mechanisms of validation.

Mass Media's Shift: Turning Private Offense into Public Spectacle

With the rise of mass media, the nature of offense began to shift gently. The printing press expanded access to information, and later, newspapers, radio, and television transformed personal grievances into public theater. Disputes that were once private became matters of national, even global, attention.

Television, in particular, carried this transformation further—turning controversy into a form of ratings gold. The news cycle started to thrive on spectacle and outrage, stoking grievances to capture attention and, in doing so, turning offense into a commodity.

> *The media doesn't just report outrage—it manufactures it, packages it, and sells it back to us for profit*

Take, for example, the Watergate scandal, which evolved from a political crisis into a national spectacle. Public outrage became both a moral statement and a commercial opportunity as media outlets learned to amplify societal grievances in a manner that resonated widely.

Self-Reflection: How has the media shaped your perception of offense? Have you noticed how certain stories invite outrage for the sake of attention? How often do you pause to question the motive behind the headlines you encounter?

Digital Amplification: Outrage Goes Viral

The advent of the internet, and particularly social media, has supercharged this evolution. Platforms originally designed for personal connection have, over time, become arenas for public outrage. Minor grievances, once resolved in quiet reflection, can now find themselves broadcast on a global stage in moments.

A clear example is the *#CancelColbert* controversy—a satirical tweet, taken out of context, that ignited a digital firestorm. This incident reflects how platforms intended to connect us have subtly shifted to amplify expressions of outrage, often rewarding displays of moral signaling over deeper, meaningful dialogue. Algorithms designed to maximize engagement now prioritize content that evokes strong emotions. In this way, offense becomes performative by design—less about restoring inner dignity and more about securing visibility and even power.

Outrage as Social Capital in the Digital Age

Today, offense has reached an extreme: outrage is no longer a spontaneous reaction but a strategic act. Social media platforms have transformed moral indignation into a kind of currency where expressions of outrage are rewarded with visibility, influence, and a semblance of moral authority.

Yet much of this outward display is not born of genuine harm but is instead a performance. Public displays of offense serve as signals of virtue, and individuals often find themselves competing for a higher moral standing in this digital marketplace of ideas. The irony is subtle but undeniable: those who most fervently claim victimhood may wield considerable influence within this ecosystem. In a curious twist, many who decry exploitation with great fervor are also those who quietly profit from it.

In this digital arena, the more one cultivates the appearance of suffering, the more influence is gathered. Outrage slowly shifts from being a heartfelt response to a commodity—traded for clicks, retweets, and influence. The digital pulpit rewards not the quiet truth of sincere emotion but the spectacle of moral indignation, transforming what was once a personal call for respect into a form of social entrepreneurship.

These platforms are not neutral channels; they are accelerants meticulously designed to fuel our inner responses. Algorithms favor content that provokes anger, as such responses drive engagement. Research indicates that posts evoking moral outrage are more likely to go viral, creating a feedback loop that reinforces habitual offense.[3]

Thus, the evolution of offense—from a private, personal signal to a public, performative act—has set the stage for something even more subtle and insidious: an addiction to outrage. As technology amplifies our reactions, what once served as a signal of moral clarity now risks becoming a compulsive behavior carefully engineered by the very systems that shape modern discourse.

Outrage as an Emotional Addiction

Before we explore how outrage rewires the brain, let us examine the cycle of addiction that it creates. Imagine a loop—a quiet yet persistent cycle of reaction, where external triggers spark moments of indignation, each one reinforced by a fleeting surge of dopamine from social validation until this pattern becomes as habitual as breathing.

Hooked on Outrage: How the Cycle Reinforces Itself

What begins as a clear, inner signal of moral awareness gradually spirals into a compulsion. Each external stimulus—each provocative headline, each contentious post—elicits a subtle burst of dopamine, reinforcing the behavior through social

---

[3] (Brady et al., 2017)

approval. Over time, that transient feeling of indignation transforms into a quiet, addictive loop—one that is repeatedly amplified by digital platforms designed to keep our attention ever engaged.

Now, having visualized the mechanics of this addiction, let us delve deeper into how this cycle becomes embedded in the brain. Understanding the biological underpinnings of this loop reveals why breaking free from outrage is not merely a matter of willpower but a process of rewiring behavior patterns shaped by reinforcement and habit.

Hijacked by Biology: How Outrage Becomes Habit

Outrage may begin as a natural, instinctive signal—a subtle response to a perceived injustice—but in our modern digital age, it often transforms into something far more insidious: a compulsion. Each burst of indignation activates the brain's reward system, setting off a biochemical loop that, through repetition, reshapes our inner circuitry. What once served as a quiet alert to protect our integrity becomes a habitual craving for external affirmation. This shift transforms the natural call for justice into a repetitive, compulsive display—a cycle of moral exhibitionism that favors reaction over reflection and superficial validation over genuine inner engagement.

The Dopamine Trap: Fueling the Cycle of Indignation

Validation-driven outrage reconfigures the brain's reward pathways. Social media platforms are finely attuned to provoke our responses and reward inflammatory content with visibility and influence. In this way, outrage is gradually transformed from a momentary emotional response into a form of social currency—persistent chase for that brief dopamine surge. Over time, the focus shifts from seeking true moral clarity to pursuing that ephemeral chemical high, forming a feedback loop that makes every digital nod of approval a reinforcing touch.

This engineered cycle is not merely theoretical; it is evident in our everyday experience. Studies reveal that expressions of moral outrage activate the brain's mesolimbic dopamine system—the same network that reinforces other forms of habitual behavior.[4] With repeated exposure, our neural circuits become more reactive, and even minor disagreements can seem to carry a weight far greater than they once did.

---

[4] (Volkow et al., 2011)

The Brain's Addiction Triggers: Fear, Reward, and Stress

To truly understand why outrage feels so irresistible, we must turn our attention inward to the very wiring of our brains. It is not solely dopamine that guides this cycle; our brains also draw on other systems that amplify our responses:

1. Amygdala Activation: The amygdala, our emotional alarm system, is naturally attuned to detect threats—whether physical, ideological, or social. In the digital realm, even a softly opposing view can stir a subtle fight-or-flight response, releasing stress hormones and heightening our sensitivity.

2. Reward Circuitry Reinforcement: Every time our expression of outrage receives validation—a like, a retweet, a supportive comment— the brain's reward system is activated, much like a gambler's pursuit of a small win. This creates a quiet loop in which the act of expressing indignation becomes its own reward.

3. Cortisol Spikes: Outrage-inducing content also raises our cortisol levels, the body's primary stress hormone. With continuous exposure, this surge of stress can leave us emotionally depleted and more sensitive, further deepening the cycle of reactive behavior.

Introspections: How does your body respond when you feel offended? Notice any sensations—a tightening in the chest, a quickened heartbeat, a subtle tension—allow these signs to be a reminder of the natural, yet now conditioned, patterns within you.

With this neurological framework, we see that what begins as a natural response to injustice transforms into a subtle yet persistent loop—one that is not only repeated but ingrained. Each episode of outrage rewards the brain, reinforcing a habit that slowly replaces genuine moral clarity with a conditioned craving for external validation. The result is a culture where the pursuit of emotional approval overshadows true, reflective engagement, and the distinction between real harm and perceived slight fades away.

The most concerning consequence of this addiction is its quiet erosion of our capacity for meaningful dialogue. When outrage becomes our default state, it no longer serves as a genuine response to injustice but transforms into a strategy for capturing attention, influence, and social currency. In a world where offense is so readily rewarded, the space for deep, thoughtful conversation diminishes under the weight of habitual indignation.

How Outrage Has Shifted from Natural Response to Compulsive Behavior

The human brain is designed for survival. Emotions like fear, anger, and indignation once served as protective signals—brief alerts prompting us to address injustice, correct wrongs, or defend our community. These responses were naturally transient and situational.

Yet, in our modern digital era, outrage is no longer a fleeting signal. It has been softly commodified, transformed into a habitual state that feeds on itself. The platforms that now connect us are meticulously designed to invite our repeated engagement. Every notification, every viral post, and every provocative headline becomes a call to react. And the pleasure of being outraged—the rush of validation—has evolved into a self-reinforcing cycle that is nearly irresistible.

The Dopamine Loop: How Moral Outrage Becomes Addictive

At the heart of this process is the brain's ancient reward system—a mechanism originally intended for survival, now tenderly repurposed by modern technology. Each surge of moral outrage releases dopamine, turning a momentary reaction into a subtle addiction. Over time, this chemical reinforcement shifts our focus from a sincere quest for justice to the pursuit of that fleeting, pleasurable high. What begins as a clear expression of indignation gradually becomes a habitual craving—a cycle where every digital applause strengthens the desire to remain in that state.

In this way, the loop of outrage does more than just invite our participation—it rewires our neural pathways, conditioning us to react more swiftly and less thoughtfully to even minor provocations. The result is a subtle but profound transformation: genuine moral clarity is gradually replaced by a compulsive need for external validation.

> *Outrage feels good in the moment—but like any addiction, it leaves you emptier than before.*

Outrage in action is not an abstract idea; it unfolds quietly every time we engage with our digital world. Social media has become an arena where outrage is both expressed and manufactured—a system that is designed, almost imperceptibly, to keep us in its cycle. This is not merely a cultural shift but a neurological transformation—one that alters our very pattern of engagement with the world.

By understanding these inner mechanisms—how our fear, reward, and stress systems intertwine—we can begin to recognize and, ultimately, disrupt the conditioned patterns that keep us locked in cycles of indignation. In the quiet spaces of awareness, we may find the strength to break free from this cycle, returning to a state of genuine moral clarity that is not dependent on external applause.

The Consequences of Manufactured Offense

When offense is no longer a private, inner experience but is transformed into a public spectacle, the effects ripple quietly through our collective consciousness. This inflation of offense—where the expression of hurt is performed rather than felt—reshapes our dialogue, diminishes the impact of genuine grievances, and softens our ability to engage in thoughtful conversation. In this cultural shift, the subtle difference between true moral transgression and the mere performance of being offended begins to blur, and our capacity for meaningful progress is diminished.

Manufactured offense, driven not by authentic harm but by the need to display moral superiority, has become a quiet contagion. It erodes the value of real suffering, corrodes our shared discourse, and fosters an atmosphere of hypersensitivity that punishes disagreement and stifles open thought.

Self-Reflection: When was the last time you allowed yourself to deeply engage with an idea that challenged your beliefs? Did you meet it with openness, or did you instinctively retreat? Consider how you might, with practice, engage with opposing viewpoints more constructively.

Before exploring further, it is essential to clarify the difference between genuine harm and what we now see as manufactured offense. This distinction illuminates the growing confusion between objective injury and subjective discomfort—a confusion that softly undermines our collective sense of justice.

When we see genuine harm—rooted in real injury and moral violation—it calls for a deep, compassionate response. In contrast, manufactured offense, often driven by subjective discomfort and performed for social recognition, risks trivializing true suffering. When minor slights are elevated to the level of major injustice, the voice of those who experience real pain can be quietly drowned out.

This delicate distinction is vital for meaningful dialogue. Without it, society risks softening the impact of true suffering by equating superficial grievances with deep injustice. Such dilution weakens the moral force necessary for social progress.

Drowning Out Real Harm: The Dilution of Genuine Grievances

One of the most immediate consequences of this shift is that genuine moral outrage loses its power. When every minor transgression is treated as if it were a profound moral emergency, the real, pressing injustices become lost in the background noise. The space for authentic grievance narrows as society struggles to distinguish between what truly harms and what is merely a transient discomfort.

When legitimate issues are intermingled with trivial offenses, the natural, deep response to injustice becomes blurred. Genuine outrage—capable of drawing attention to significant social wrongs and inspiring real change—is softened, reduced to a mere echo amid a multitude of manufactured complaints.

Silencing Dissent: The Death of Open Discourse

Another significant consequence of this culture of manufactured offense is the gradual erosion of open dialogue. A vibrant society depends on the free exchange of ideas and the willingness to engage with perspectives that may unsettle our inner calm.

However, when every expression of disagreement is swiftly interpreted as a personal attack, the space for true conversation diminishes. The beauty of diverse thought is quietly stifled. The fear of causing offense leads many to withhold their honest views, and what remains is soft but pervasive self-censorship. Universities and public forums once haven for robust exploration of ideas, now sometimes become environments where the pursuit of truth is hindered by the need to avoid conflict.

A culture obsessed with being offended does not create safer spaces—it creates silent ones.

The Fragility Trap: Rising Hypersensitivity in Society

Perhaps the most insidious consequence of manufactured offense is the cultivation of hypersensitivity—a state in which even a small discomfort is perceived as a deep moral transgression. In such a climate, individuals become emotionally fragile, feeling as though any challenge or differing opinion is a threat to their very being.

This hypersensitivity is not true compassion but rather a tender, defensive reaction that discourages growth and honest dialogue. Research suggests that when people are continuously sheltered from discomfort, their capacity for resilience softens, making it harder to face real adversity. Concepts like "safe spaces" and "trigger warnings," while born from genuine care, may inadvertently encourage avoidance of challenging ideas, limiting our inner strength and creativity.

> *The more fragile we become, the less resilient we are. And a world without resilience crumbles at the first sign of discomfort.*

The cumulative effect of these shifts is profound. Manufactured offense not only diminishes the impact of real harm but also silences the honest exchange of ideas and fosters an emotional fragility that leaves society less capable of handling complexity and dissent.

"The degree of one's emotions varies inversely with one's knowledge of the facts." — Bertrand Russell

In embracing this awareness, we learn that the future of open dialogue and intellectual freedom depends on our ability to discern true injustice from transient discomfort. Recognizing and resisting the soft pull of manufactured offense may help us restore the space for genuine compassion and thoughtful engagement—a quiet step toward reclaiming the integrity of our collective moral voice.

Why Understanding Offense Matters

We no longer live in a quiet world where offense is a personal matter. Today, it has become a public performance—a currency of influence and a subtle tool of power that shapes our collective dialogue. To truly understand offense is not merely to manage our discomfort but to recognize its role in redefining the boundaries of intellectual freedom, social unity, and inner resilience.

The expression of being offended is not just an emotional reaction; it has evolved into a public display. Genuine moral conviction, born of an inner knowing and deep integrity, stands in quiet contrast to the hollow performance that often dominates our discourse. When offense is used as a tool for self-promotion, it weakens the very fabric of open dialogue. It is the difference between an honest, heartfelt response to injustice and a loud declaration meant to attract fleeting validation.

True offense arises when one's deeply held values or sense of dignity is genuinely transgressed—a call for inner reflection and, when necessary, a prompt for meaningful action. This authentic reaction, grounded in personal integrity, invites us to listen to the quiet voice within. Yet, when our hurt becomes performative, it transforms into a social strategy—a way to signal moral superiority rather than to seek understanding.

***Self-Reflection**, consider the thin line between integrity and performance. Ask yourself: Is your own sense of being offended a true reflection of your inner truth, or has it become a performance shaped by external expectations?*

In moments of sincere hurt, we are invited to pause, look inward, and allow our natural wisdom to guide us. Authentic offense leads to compassion and constructive dialogue, while performative outrage only deepens the noise, distancing us from our inner stillness.

The consequences of living in a state of perpetual offense extend far beyond personal discomfort. Constant indignation not only corrodes our capacity for clear thinking but also diminishes our collective ability to engage in open, honest conversation. When every slight is magnified into a moral emergency, the space for genuine discourse gradually shrinks, and our inner capacity for empathy and resilience begins to wane.

In reclaiming our inner freedom, we learn that true dialogue—rich in complexity and compassion—requires us to distinguish between what is deeply harmful and what is merely transient discomfort. By letting go of the need to perform our indignation for the world, we open the possibility for a more profound connection with ourselves and others—a space where intellectual freedom and authentic compassion can flourish.

Self-Reflection: *Next time you feel offended, ask yourself: Is this reaction guiding me toward truth, or am I simply playing my part in the performance?*

Am I seeking resolution, or am I seeking attention? True strength lies not in announcing offense, but in learning when to let go. The question is: Are you willing to break the cycle?

When we learn to embrace the quiet strength of our inner truth, we rediscover that real power lies not in being perpetually offended but in cultivating the calm, steady presence of true integrity.

In this space of reflection, we begin to see that the future of our public discourse—and indeed, our inner well-being—depends on our ability to move beyond the compulsive need for external affirmation. True freedom is found in the silence of the heart, where offense is met not with a clamor for attention but with the peaceful understanding that all things are transient.

> *Real strength is not found in being perpetually offended. It is found in knowing when to let go.*

Outrage Addiction Insight

Why does being offended feel like a personal attack?

Neuroscience research reveals that perceived threats activate the amygdala, triggering a fight-or-flight response and releasing stress hormones like cortisol and adrenaline.[1] This heightened state of arousal reinforces a defensive stance, making outrage feel both necessary and rewarding. Each time you react to perceived offense, your brain receives a dopamine hit, strengthening the addictive cycle of being offended.[2]

---

[1] *LeDoux, 2000*
[2] *Sapolsky, 2004*

Chapter Two

The Need for Moral Superiority

"Moral indignation is jealousy with a halo."

— H.G. Wells

The Quest for Moral Superiority

When did morality stop being about what we do in silence—and start being about what we can prove to the world? Today, being good is no longer enough; you must be seen as good. And in this shift, the quiet depth of true virtue has been replaced by the loud performance of moral superiority.

Morality, once an intimate truth, is now paraded before the world—a spectacle seeking not genuine reflection but the fleeting warmth of validation and applause. We live in a culture where being seen as good seems to matter more than the quiet essence of goodness itself.[1]

Here lies an uncomfortable truth: modern morality has shifted. It is no longer about living with deep inner conviction; it has become about being seen having that conviction. Ethics once held tenderly in the privacy of personal conscience, are now performed on a public stage. We no longer strive simply to be good—we strive to appear good. And in that pursuit, the true essence of integrity is often the first to fade away.

> *The deep yearning to be seen as virtuous can sometimes obscure the silent depth of true goodness.*

---

[1] *Wit & Wisdom. The Week, (1402), 19.*

The Rise of Moral Exhibitionism

We no longer live in a world of quiet conviction. We live in a world of moral theater—a stage where every expression of virtue is carefully curated for public approval. The rise of social media has not just amplified moral posturing; it has made it expected. Here, morality is not so much about the substance of our inner being as it is about a performance for the world. Every tweet, every post, and every public statement becomes an opportunity to present ourselves as enlightened, compassionate, or "woke," regardless of whether these expressions are supported by deep, meaningful action.

> *Supporting a cause in quiet conviction is often overshadowed by the urge to display it outwardly.*

This tendency, what might be called moral exhibitionism, arises from the need for external recognition. In a state of inner stillness, supporting a cause in silence holds profound power. Yet today, to prove one's virtue, we feel compelled to display it openly. The more we reveal, the more social reward we seek. Digital algorithms, in their own way, amplify these outward performances—pushing the loudest expressions to the forefront, often regardless of their inner depth. In this theater of public display, the quiet truth is easily lost, and the value of genuine sincerity is overshadowed by the glow of visibility.

The irony is clear: in the pursuit of perceived moral superiority, many become more absorbed in the appearance of virtue than in the cultivation of true inner integrity.

Self-Reflection: When did you last feel compelled to broadcast your moral beliefs? Was it an expression of inner conviction or merely a yearning for external validation?

The Addictive High of Moral Validation

There is a subtle yet powerful allure in moral posturing. It is not simply a matter of ego—it is also a biological process at work. Neuroscience teaches us that public expressions of outrage trigger the brain's reward system, releasing dopamine—the same energy that underlies other forms of addiction. Moral outrage is the new sugar rush. Each like, each share, each moment of validation hits the brain like a quick dose of dopamine—fast, addictive, and ultimately empty. But like any addiction, the highs fade, and the craving grows. What started as conviction becomes compulsion.

> *Each outburst of outrage may seem like moral clarity, yet it often serves as a fleeting rush—a subtle craving for external affirmation that distracts us from our inner stillness.*

When we seek validation from the outer world, what begins as a moment of sincere conviction can be overtaken by the rush for recognition. In this way, our moral clarity may dissolve into compulsive performance, and the applause that once felt empowering gradually becomes a prison of expectation.

Consider the loop: a moral declaration leads to social validation; validation triggers a dopamine surge; that surge reinforces our outward behavior, drawing us back into the cycle. This is the subtle dance of moral superiority—a cycle that transforms genuine inner conviction into a compulsive performance.

The Distinction Between Genuine Morality and Performance

It is essential to discern the difference between true morality and its performative counterpart. True morality is rooted in quiet, consistent action—a deep inner conviction that guides us even when no one is watching. In contrast, performative virtue is a display crafted for the world's approval—a spectacle that seeks external validation rather than emanating from an inner knowing.

This difference is particularly evident in our digital age. One may tweet passionately about social justice without ever engaging in the heartfelt work that such causes require. Popular slogans and hashtags fill our screens, yet they often lack the depth of true understanding or the commitment of genuine action. This is the nature of virtue signaling—the outer appearance of morality, unburdened by the weight of sincere engagement.

Recognizing this distinction is vital. While performative outrage may appear harmless, it diminishes the profound nature of our shared concerns. It reduces complex issues to surface-level displays and fosters a culture in which appearances overshadow the quiet truth of our being. In this way, the genuine effort for social change is lost amid the clamor of spectacle.

When society is increasingly captivated by moral exhibitionism, the true challenge is not to be seen as virtuous but to live from a deep inner virtue—quietly, consistently, without the need for applause. Only when we become aware of the seductive pull of moral superiority can we begin to reclaim the authenticity of our true nature.

∞∞∞

In today's hyper-visible society, morality has shifted from being an inner, quiet guide to becoming a public performance. The desire for moral superiority often arises not from deep personal conviction but from the yearning for external validation. Now, the appearance of being "good" holds far more weight than the simple yet profound act of living virtuously.

Virtue Signaling: The Performance of Morality

There is a quiet irony in our modern moral dialogue. Often, those who appear most righteous are not necessarily those with the deepest inner truth. In the unfolding theater of contemporary outrage, virtue signaling has become the center stage—a performance in which expressions of moral concern are shared not solely to create meaningful change but to affirm one's personal standing. It is, in essence, morality as performance art—a display in which external appearances take precedence over the silent substance of being, and the loudest declarations of virtue may conceal the lightness of inner conviction.

What Is Virtue Signaling?

Virtue signaling can be likened to a momentary indulgence—offering instant gratification yet leaving the deeper nourishment of true virtue unfulfilled.

> *Virtue signaling is the moral equivalent of fast food: easy to consume, instantly gratifying, and devoid of substance.*

In its true form, virtue signaling is not the clear expression of moral insight; it is a kind of moral theater. It is less about transforming the world and more about drawing applause from the crowd. In this economy of collective outrage, the depth of sincerity is often set aside while the desire for visibility takes its place.

It is not about making a tangible difference but about being seen as caring and about being perceived as standing on the "right side" of an issue. While many genuinely feel a connection to the causes they champion, often, the subtle motivation is less about deep principle and more about nurturing one's reputation. The longing to be recognized as virtuous can, in many ways, overshadow the impulse for truly meaningful action.

Virtue Signaling Spectrum

Not all virtue is real. Some of it is theater. Imagine a Moral Integrity Scale—on one end, quiet, consistent action. On the other, hollow virtue signaling designed for applause. Where do your actions truly fall? This visual guide reminds us that not every moral display is empty. It offers us the opportunity to discern the difference between heartfelt ethical living and the superficial show of virtue.

The Illusion of Moral Credibility

Virtue signaling often reveals a surface-level expression of morality. In contrast to true advocacy—which calls forth tangible actions, sacrifice, and deep engagement—virtue signaling offers a kind of moral credit without significant inner cost. A tweet, a hashtag, a carefully rehearsed gesture—each requires little effort yet yields an immediate social reward. They are much like moral fast food: instantly satisfying but lacking in lasting nourishment.

Why Is It Dangerous?

The danger lies in the way this behavior can subtly distort our moral discourse. Nuanced causes, deserving of deep reflection and thoughtful action, are sometimes reduced to simple slogans. Moreover, activism in this mode becomes a race for visibility rather than a sincere journey toward justice. When the authenticity of these gestures is questioned, dissent may be met with swift labeling—dismissing alternative perspectives as indifferent or even complicit—and thereby quieting a deeper conversation.

The Psychology Behind Virtue Signaling

The allure of virtue signaling is deeply interwoven with a fundamental human need: the need for connection and social validation. We are naturally inclined toward togetherness, and the desire for approval is woven into our very being.

The Social Validation Trap

Public expressions of our morality serve as signals—quiet affirmations of our alignment with what is considered the "right" path. Yet, these signals also work to enhance our social standing and reputation.[2]

The Reward System in Overdrive

On a neurological level, the act of virtue signaling taps into our brain's reward system. Every time an expression of moral concern garners a like, a retweet, or a supportive comment, a surge of dopamine is released. This fleeting reward encourages us to repeat these behaviors.[3] Over time, the cycle continues not solely from deep inner conviction but from the soft allure of external validation.

Crafting the Public Persona

This pattern is closely linked with what we know as impression management—the subtle, unconscious drive to shape how we are seen by others.[4] In our digital age, sharing opinions becomes less an expression of inner truth and more an artful curation of a moral identity. Our personal brand now extends beyond professional aspirations into a persistent endeavor to appear virtuous.

The Cost of Superficial Validation

Yet, there is a price for this pursuit of validation. When the performance of virtue is detached from meaningful action, our ethics risk becoming little more than an empty display—a quest for social capital rather than a path toward genuine transformation.

> *"When our focus rests solely on how virtue appears to others, the quiet essence of true goodness may gently fade away."*

Examples of Virtue Signaling in Modern Culture

The phenomenon of virtue signaling is not confined to the quiet corners of the internet; it touches every part of our mainstream culture, influencing how individuals, corporations, and even governments relate to social issues. This pattern creates a landscape where moral posturing is sometimes mistaken for heartfelt activism.

---

[2] *Jordan, Sommers, Bloom, & Rand, 2016*
[3] *(Schultz, 2016).*
[4] *(Leary & Kowalski, 1990).*

Social Media Activism That Prioritizes Visibility Over Action.

On platforms such as Twitter and Instagram, we see a tendency for activism to take the form of performance. A hashtag or a symbol shared during global events can sometimes replace deeper engagement. In the rush to be part of a movement, the risk is that complex issues are reduced to transient trends, and their deeper messages become obscured by fleeting gestures.

Public Statements of Solidarity That Lack Follow-Through

The corporate world, too, participates in this dance of superficial solidarity. Companies often issue statements in support of progressive causes during moments of social change—especially when silence might invite criticism. Yet, these declarations frequently lack the substance of follow-through. Such expressions, more concerned with maintaining a favorable image than with enacting real change, reveal a disconnect between what is said and what is done.

Outrage Expressed Over Issues Disconnected from Personal Stakes

Another quiet observation is that sometimes we see individuals expressing outrage over issues that do not directly touch their lives. This is not always a true outpouring of empathy but rather a form of moral exhibitionism. In swiftly condemning distant practices or decisions, the impulse may arise more from a desire to project moral authority than from genuine understanding. It is an act that allows one to appear enlightened, even if it lacks the depth of real engagement.

Self-Reflection: *do your public declarations of support arise from genuine commitment, or are they curated for the sake of external approval?*

Virtue signaling, therefore, is more than an individual habit—it is a cultural phenomenon that diminishes the true depth of moral dialogue. It reduces the spirit of activism to performance and cultivates a climate where the appearance of virtue can overshadow the essence of authentic ethical responsibility. Recognizing this dynamic is essential not only to grasp the superficial nature of such modern morality but also to reclaim the integrity of our public discourse in a society increasingly enchanted by the spectacle of righteousness.

∞∞∞∞

Virtue signaling transforms morality into a performance—valuing appearances over genuine action. Though it may seem harmless, this shallow form of engagement dilutes the power of true activism, reduces complex issues to mere gestures, and fosters a culture where reputation overshadows heartfelt ethical responsibility. In today's hyper-connected world, this performance finds its richest expression online—where outrage is a currency, and digital platforms reward those who best master the art of display.

The Role of Social Media in Amplifying Virtue Signaling

In our increasingly digital age, social media has become a modern coliseum—a vast arena where public displays of morality are not only common but quietly rewarded with likes, shares, and a transient sense of social esteem. Here, virtue signaling is no longer an occasional act; it has evolved into a continual performance where individuals, perhaps unknowingly, compete for moral prominence on a global stage. In this digital landscape, outrage has become industrialized—a cultural obsession that, in many ways, mirrors a profitable business model.

The Algorithm of Outrage

It is not by chance that outrage finds fertile ground online. Platforms such as Twitter, Facebook, and Instagram are not neutral spaces for a simple exchange of ideas. They are finely tuned instruments designed to maximize engagement, where nothing captures attention quite like the surge of moral indignation. The algorithms that govern these platforms prioritize content that evokes strong emotional responses—anger, indignation—because such feelings keep us engaged. In essence, these digital mechanisms serve as accelerants, allowing outrage to flourish until it overshadows quiet reflection and softens the voice of dissent.

> *In the digital arena, what is exchanged is not the quiet truth of our being, but the clamor of outrage that captures fleeting attention.*

A visual flowchart might gently remind us how these algorithms function, revealing the feedback loop that transforms indignation into a kind of viral currency.

Echo Chambers and the Race for Moral High Ground

Beyond mere exposure, these algorithms create echo chambers—digital spaces where we encounter opinions that mirror our own. Within these ideological bubbles, the pursuit of moral high ground grows ever more intense. The more we conform to the prevailing narrative and amplify it with heightened emotion, the more validation we receive. This can lead to a quiet escalation, where moderate views are gradually silenced by increasingly extreme positions. In these online communities, the most impassioned voices often gain traction—not because they offer deeper wisdom but because they stir the strongest emotional reactions.

One might pause and ask, "How often do you truly encounter differing perspectives in your digital space? What might that say about the nature of your online environment?"

Public Validation as Currency

On these digital platforms, public validation has become a subtle currency. Every like, share, retweet, or supportive comment serves as a small affirmation—a nod that our moral expressions are acknowledged. These micro-rewards activate the brain's natural reward system, inviting us to repeat our behavior. Over time, this creates a feedback loop where the expression of moral outrage invites further validation. As a result, our engagement with complex moral issues can be overshadowed by a rush for external approval—a dependence on public affirmation that quietly diminishes our inner sense of self-worth.

In such an environment, morality risks becoming transactional—a means to accumulate social capital rather than a reflection of our deepest integrity. The cultural landscape shifts subtly, favoring the spectacle of virtue over the quiet, consistent work of inner transformation.

Social media has not simply amplified virtue signaling—it has redefined it. These digital spaces reward outrage and incentivize extremism, turning moral exhibition into a kind of currency in the marketplace of attention. To understand the nature of modern outrage, we must recognize how these structures have, in their own way, shaped and even commodified our basic moral instincts.

Maya Angelou said, "There is a very fine line between loving life and being greedy for it." In this context, we are invited to see that the pursuit of public validation can easily shift from a simple expression of life's goodness into a relentless craving for more.

∞∞∞

Social media thrives on the energy of outrage, encouraging us to seek validation through public displays of indignation. The algorithm-driven race for attention tends to reward extremism over nuance, transforming morality into a competitive and sometimes addictive performance. Yet, within this digital dance, there remains a call to return to quiet reflection—a reminder to reconnect with the inner compass of genuine integrity.

The Psychology of Moral Superiority

There is a subtle inner dynamic at work when we feel compelled to display our moral convictions—a quiet interplay between the ego, the fear of being isolated, and the natural cycles of reward within our nervous system. Beneath every public expression of indignation, there lies a delicate blend of inner longing for affirmation and the deep-seated need to belong.

Ego Validation: Nurturing the Illusion of Superiority

At the heart of this phenomenon is the ego, which gently seeks confirmation from the outer world. Each public display of moral outrage serves as a small offering to that inner part of ourselves, reinforcing a sense of superiority. Research on self-enhancement bias reminds us that we often view ourselves in an overly favorable light.[5]. Yet, when our actions are driven primarily by the need to be seen as virtuous, they may lose their inner depth. In such moments, what appears as moral clarity is often a delicate illusion—a quiet righteousness that is more about the appearance of virtue than about genuine inner conviction.

> *When the call for virtue grows too loud, the gentle strength of genuine conviction may be lost.*

Belonging at a Cost: The Fear of Isolation

Our longing to be part of a community is as old as humanity itself. Evolution taught us that belonging was essential for survival and today, that instinct softly whispers through our social interactions.[6] In our modern age, silence can be mistakenly read as detachment, prompting us to align our voices with the majority.

---

[5] *Sedikides* & Gregg, 2008
[6] *Baumeister & Leary, 1995*

This pressure can lead to a performance of conformity, where the desire to be accepted overshadows the quiet voice of authentic thought. In such environments, the rich tapestry of diverse ideas is at risk of being woven into a single, uniform narrative, and the space for genuine dialogue begins to narrow.

The Addictive High of Moral Validation

There is a subtle allure in the act of sharing our moral views with the world. Neuroscience shows us that when we express our outrage publicly, our brains release dopamine—the same surge that underlies other forms of addiction.[7] Each like, share, or supportive comment becomes a small, ephemeral gift that comforts the ego. Over time, this external validation can form a cycle, drawing us into a pattern of seeking approval rather than nurturing our inner wisdom. What begins as a sincere expression of concern may gradually be transformed by this craving for recognition, leaving behind an echo of emptiness once the applause fades.

> *The craving for external affirmation can become as compelling as any habit, drawing us away from the stillness of true being.*

The Hidden Cost: The Erosion of Authenticity

When every moral stance becomes a performance, we risk losing touch with our true essence. The constant quest for external affirmation can blur the line between what we deeply believe and what we display for others. Over time, this subtle shift can lead to a loss of authenticity, as our inner compass is replaced by the need for social validation. One might gently ask: Are our values truly our own, or have they become borrowed reflections shaped by the yearning for approval?

In the early stages, the rush of validation may feel empowering—a tender reminder that our inner light is recognized. Yet, as this pattern deepens, the need for external confirmation can overshadow quiet introspection. Our identity begins to depend on the fleeting reactions of others rather than on the steady, inner knowing that comes from within. The result is a hollow sense of self—a moral identity constructed on transient applause rather than on enduring authenticity.

Beyond this loss of inner integrity, there is an emotional toll. The constant performance of outrage, over time, can lead to a persistent exhaustion—a quiet

---

burnout that leaves us feeling disconnected from the causes we once held dear. This is not true empathy; it is a weariness born from the unending chase for external approval.

> *In its ceaseless outpouring, outrage may quietly leave the well of genuine empathy barren.*

When we let go of the incessant urge to perform our morality, we open the space for true, heartfelt connection and a deeper, more resilient compassion.

Self-Reflection: How might our relationships or sense of self shift if we allowed our values to emerge from a place of quiet inner strength, rather than from a need for recognition?

The Dual Consequence: A Hollow Self and Emotional Exhaustion

The quiet cost of this cycle is profound. When our identity is tied to the endless pursuit of moral validation, both our authenticity and our emotional vitality begin to wane. Over time, this can lead to a public landscape filled not with thoughtful engagement, but with hollow declarations—a chorus of voices echoing without depth.

∞∞∞∞

Moral superiority is nourished by three powerful forces: the need for ego validation, the innate fear of exclusion, and the addictive pull of social approval. These forces, when unexamined, trap us in a cycle where genuine reflection is quietly eroded, and meaningful discourse is replaced by a performance of outrage. The world is watching. But does that mean you must always perform? What if you stopped proving your morality and simply lived it? Real virtue needs no audience. The only question is: Are you willing to live it when no one is looking.

Case Studies: When Moral Superiority Backfires

In the arena of public perception, the applause that once elevated our spirit can, in an instant, transform into the weight of judgment. In this unfolding drama of collective consciousness, moral superiority may serve both as a pedestal and as the guillotine—a reminder that what we exhibit externally is ever-shifting and transient.

> *The applause of our shared outrage may be fleeting, for it can just as swiftly become the source of our downfall.*

In a society that thrives on public displays of morality, the pedestal of virtue signaling is as delicate as it is precarious. Built on the ever-changing sands of public opinion, this performance of righteousness can collapse without warning. Those who seem to soar highest on the wings of public approval may also be those most vulnerable to a sudden fall.

Virtue Signaling Leading to Backlash

Hypocrisy Unveiled: Jussie Smollett and the Perils of Manufactured Victimhood

In January 2019, the public was stirred by the story of actor Jussie Smollett, who claimed to have suffered a racially charged hate crime. In the ensuing tidal wave of compassion and solidarity, countless voices rose in unison, affirming their own moral alignment. Yet, as the truth emerged—that the incident had been orchestrated for personal gain—a profound disillusionment settled in. The collective outpouring of support that had once seemed so genuine now revealed the fragility of a system built on performative outrage. Here, the allure of victimhood as a source of power was laid bare, reminding us that when self-interest is clothed in virtue, the collapse is both inevitable and deeply transformative.

Cancel Culture Cannibalism: J.K. Rowling and the Movement That Turned on Its Own

Consider the case of J.K. Rowling, whose celebrated contributions once united hearts through her tales of inclusivity. When her views on gender identity sparked fierce public debate in 2020, the same culture that had once embraced her turned with swift intensity. In the blink of an eye, the collective consciousness redefined her narrative, exiling her from the moral high ground she had helped to create. Her experience serves as a meditative reminder: in a realm where ideological conformity is prized above all, even those who once nurtured the spirit of inclusion can find themselves cast into isolation. This cautionary tale gently asks: what is the cost when dissent is met not with dialogue, but with silent, sweeping exclusion?

The Psychological Fallout of Moral Exhibitionism

Beyond these public episodes lies the quieter, more personal realm of emotional consequence. For those caught in the cycle of moral posturing—such as public figures like Chrissy Teigen—the toll can be profound. When past missteps resurface under the relentless gaze of the public, the pressure to maintain a flawless moral façade can lead to deep inner turmoil. The very platform that once elevated their sense of purpose becomes a source of enduring anxiety and self-doubt. The emotional collapse that follows is not merely a matter of public shame; it is a reminder that the hunger for external validation can leave the heart empty, and the spirit fatigued.

Lessons from Failed Virtue Signaling

When morality becomes a performance, it is like a house of cards built on ephemeral applause. Public declarations of virtue without genuine inner alignment are fragile, and when exposed as hollow, the backlash is swift and merciless. In this delicate interplay, the same crowd that once celebrated our declarations may soon be the one that witnesses our downfall. This is the paradox of our time: the louder we project our moral declarations, the sharper the fall may be when authenticity is found wanting.

> **Superficial Morality is Unsustainable:** Public displays that lack deep conviction crumble under scrutiny.
>
> **Outrage Culture Devours Its Own:** No one remains immune from the shifting gaze of public judgment.
>
> **The Cost of Living for Validation:** The relentless pursuit of external approval may lead to profound inner disconnection.

In the silent court of public opinion, today's hero can swiftly become tomorrow's cautionary tale. True integrity does not seek the clamor of applause; it resides quietly in the depths of being, nurtured by consistent, heartfelt conviction.

> *"True moral integrity isn't loud—it's quiet, consistent, and asks for no applause."*

Performative outrage is a fragile construct—built on fleeting approval and ever-changing public sentiment. Pursue moral superiority too long on this unstable foundation, and the very system that once exalted you may ultimately turn away, leaving behind a void where genuine integrity once resided. In the quiet spaces of inner reflection, we find that true virtue is not proclaimed—it is simply lived.

"Hypocrisy: prejudice with a halo."
— *Ambrose Bierce*

Outrage Addiction Insight

Why does signaling moral superiority feel rewarding?

Research shows that acts of moral posturing stimulate the brain's reward system, releasing dopamine when social approval is received.[1] This creates a compulsive loop of validation-seeking behavior, where the reward comes not from doing good but from being recognized for appearing morally superior.[2]

---

[1] *Rothschild & Keefer, 2017*
[2] *Tomasello & Vaish, 2013*

We'd Love to Hear From You!

Thank you so much for reading this book-it means the world to me. If you found it helpful, inspiring, or just enjoyable, would you take a moment to leave a review? Your feedback not only helps others but also keeps me motivated to create more valuable content for you.

Here's how you can leave a review:

1. Scan the QR code on this page to go directly to the author's page.

2. Or, visit your Amazon Orders page, find this book, and click "Write a Product Review."

Your kind words make a big difference.
Thank you for your support!

Chapter Three

The Paradox of Empathy

"Empathy without boundaries is self-destruction."

— Silvy Khoucasian

The Essence of Empathy:
Witnessing vs. Absorbing

Why does empathy sometimes feel light and freeing, yet other times heavy and exhausting? The difference is this: true empathy witnesses, while false empathy absorbs. It is not something one does, but something one allows.

Yet, the mind distorts it. It grasps at suffering, makes it personal, turns it into identity. The simple act of witnessing is replaced by absorption—by the unconscious belief that to feel another's pain, one must take it on as their own.

But pain is not healed by adding more pain.

True empathy is not suffering—it is spaciousness. The more suffering you take on, the less present you become. The mind tells you that to care, you must carry pain. But real compassion does not weigh you down—it frees you

> *True empathy does not weigh you down—it sets you free.*

To witness suffering is not to merge with it, but to remain present with it.

To absorb suffering is to become trapped within it.

This is the difference between awareness and identification.

The Stillness of Witnessing

Can you hold space for suffering without becoming it? True presence does not resist pain, nor does it cling to it. It simply allows it to be. It is to be fully present with what is, without adding to it, without making it part of the mind's narrative.

The tree does not collapse under the weight of the storm. It bends, it moves, but it remains rooted.

Clarity is not in suffering but in stillness. When you are fully present, suffering passes through you, but it does not stay—it does not become who you are.

The stillness of witnessing is the deepest form of empathy. It is not reactive. It does not seek to fix, to change, to control. It is simply there.

It says: I see you. I hear you. I am here.

It does not say: I must suffer for you, I must prove my concern, I must take on your pain as my own.

The Illusion of Absorbing Suffering

The mind is always searching for something to attach itself to, something to define itself by. And so, it turns empathy into identity.

It says: If I feel their pain, then I am good.

It says: If I suffer enough, then I am compassionate.

But suffering cannot heal suffering. To take on another's pain does not lighten their burden; it only adds to the weight of suffering in the world. When empathy is tied to identity, it is no longer about the other—it is about the self.

> *Over time, it is no longer about those who suffer—it is about maintaining the feeling of being good.*

This is why the mind clings to outrage, why it seeks suffering to react to. It is not because it wishes to relieve pain, but because it wishes to define itself through it.

The deeper truth is this: one cannot help another by drowning with them.

Presence lifts. Identification pulls down.

> *"You cannot lift another while sinking yourself."*

From Absorption to Awareness

The shift from absorbing to witnessing is a shift from unconsciousness to awareness. It is the recognition that empathy does not require suffering—only presence. A mirror does not become what it reflects. True empathy is the same—it holds, but it does not absorb.

This is true compassion.

It is not resistance, nor detachment. It is not absorption, nor avoidance. It is the space in between—the open awareness that sees, understands, and remains.

When suffering arises, be with it. Let it pass through you as wind passes through an open window. Do not close the window. Do not grasp at the wind.

Simply witness.

◦◦◦◦◦

Empathy is not the absorption of suffering, but the presence with it. When you witness, you remain open. When you absorb, you become lost. You do not help by drowning with them. You help by staying still, by being the presence in which suffering dissolves.

The Empathy Trap: When Caring Turns into an Addiction

What if the way you've been taught to care is actually harming you? The more you make suffering your own, the less you can help. Pain does not lift—only presence does. If you drown in suffering, you do not save others. You disappear with them. But there is a point at which empathy shifts from presence to possession, from seeing suffering to absorbing it as our own. And when this happens, empathy no longer serves as a bridge to understanding—it becomes a weight, dragging both the observer and the observed deeper into pain.

This is the trap of empathy addiction. The mind convinces us that the more suffering we internalize, the more compassionate we are. That to truly help, we must feel the pain ourselves. But this is not compassion—it is self-attachment. And self-attachment, no matter how noble it appears, is still attachment.

> *Like any addiction, the need to prove one's empathy begins subtly—with validation, with outrage, with a rush of feeling good.*

The Illusion of "Caring More"

Have you ever felt the need to prove your compassion? To show the world how deeply you feel? The mind convinces us that more suffering means more caring, but true empathy is not measured in pain.

The mind reacts. It doesn't just register the pain—it claims it.

This is my suffering too.

I must feel this fully, or I am not a good person.

If I take this on, I am proving that I care.

Who are you without your suffering? If pain is the proof of your compassion, what remains when it is gone? This is the ego at work—co-opting empathy and turning it into a measure of identity.

A person might believe that feeling more deeply makes them more virtuous. That their pain on behalf of others makes them morally superior to those who do not display such distress. But what does this accomplish? If anything, it deepens suffering rather than alleviating it. Instead of bringing clarity, over-identification leads to emotional indulgence—a cycle in which suffering feeds the self-image rather than healing the situation.

Have you ever felt the pull to prove your compassion? To display outrage, sorrow, or deep concern, not because it changes anything, but because it affirms something in you? This is the illusion of "caring more." It is not rooted in true presence, but in the mind's need to attach itself to suffering to define itself. And this is where empathy transforms from an act of connection into a form of self-identification.

Compassion Fatigue: When Empathy Becomes Too Much

Can you truly help another if you are drowning in their pain? When empathy is hijacked by identification, it ceases to be a gift and becomes a burden.

When suffering is no longer witnessed but absorbed, we become lost in it. Instead of being able to hold space for another's pain, we become overwhelmed by our own emotions—grief, anger, despair. This is why those who deeply internalize the suffering of others often feel paralyzed, unable to take meaningful action.

- The humanitarian worker who burns out—not from doing too much, but from feeling too much.

- The activist who once fought for change, but is now drowning in emotional exhaustion.

- The person who sees injustice everywhere, but is so overwhelmed that they do nothing at all.

Empathy, when hijacked by the ego, stops being an act of service and becomes a source of self-inflicted suffering. The mind is caught in an endless loop: the more pain it takes on, the more real and righteous it feels. But in this cycle, the actual suffering remains unchanged.

This is why excessive empathy does not make one more compassionate—it makes one emotionally drained.

Can you see how suffering is compounded by identification? How the attempt to "feel more" does not relieve pain, but multiplies it?

> *The mind convinces you that carrying more pain makes you good. But drowning in suffering does not make you compassionate—it makes you disappear.*

The Burden of Empathy: When Feeling Too Much Becomes a Trap

How much pain can one person carry before they break? The world convinces you that you must bear it all, but the truth is: taking on suffering does not end it—it only spreads it.

Those who have made empathy their burden rather than their awareness reach a threshold where they can no longer function.

- The person who once cared deeply about social issues, but now feels numb, disillusioned, or resentful.

- The individual who engages in endless cycles of outrage, but cannot remember the last time they felt peace.

– The empath who has absorbed so much external pain that they have lost connection with their own joy.

This is not compassion. This is emotional depletion.

The mind convinces you that carrying more pain makes you good. But how can you lift another if you are drowning yourself?

In psychological research, this phenomenon is known as empathy overload or compassion fatigue. Studies show that when individuals are exposed to too much suffering—especially through constant media consumption—the brain enters a state of chronic stress. The amygdala, the region responsible for processing emotions, remains in a heightened state of reactivity. The body floods with cortisol. Over time, this results in emotional shutdown—a defensive mechanism where the mind, unable to sustain endless grief, simply disconnects.

And so the paradox completes itself: the desire to feel more leads to feeling nothing at all.

"Compassion without wisdom is dangerous."

— Sadhguru

Breaking Free from the Trap of Empathy Addiction

What if you could care deeply without being consumed? The mind believes pain is proof of love, but true love does not demand suffering—it demands presence.

To help others, one does not need to carry their suffering—one only needs to be present. True empathy does not attach. It does not absorb, claim, or perform. It simply sees.

The solution is not detachment or apathy. It is not about feeling less. It is about shifting from identification to awareness:

– Compassion is seeing suffering and offering presence.

– Over-identification is making suffering your own and becoming emotionally depleted.

The world does not need more suffering—it needs more clarity. Real change does not come from carrying pain but from standing outside of it.

It is not a lack of feeling. It is the presence of wisdom.

Stop and Consider: *Are you witnessing, or are you absorbing?*

The difference is everything. Let empathy pass through you, not weigh upon you. You cannot be a light for others while carrying darkness within yourself. Empathy that flows through you heals; empathy that clings to you drains.

Can you witness pain without the ego rushing to claim it? Can you be fully present with suffering, without becoming lost in it?

This is true empathy. This is the difference between being consumed by pain and being a space in which pain can dissolve.

Empathy on Display: The Performance Trap

Empathy that needs an audience is not empathy—it is self-concern dressed as care. In a world obsessed with performance, even kindness has become a currency—spent in pursuit of validation rather than connection. Like the breath, like the beating of the heart, it arises naturally when one is present.

And yet, when the mind is caught in identification, even empathy becomes something else—a role to play, a performance to perfect, a way of proving one's own goodness to the world.

This is the shift: from witnessing to performing, from simply being with suffering to needing others to see that we care.

True empathy is lost when presence is replaced by the need for validation.

The Business of Outrage: How Empathy Became a Social Currency

The ego, always searching for affirmation, transforms the natural impulse to care into a social currency.

Rather than simply holding space for another's experience, one begins to seek confirmation: Am I caring enough? Am I being seen as compassionate? The act of witnessing suffering is no longer enough—one must be recognized for having witnessed it.

This is why suffering, once private, is now displayed.

Grief is posted, outrage is announced, and acts of compassion are made visible—not necessarily because they are false, but because they have become entangled with the need for social recognition.

> *Empathy does not need an audience. If it does, it is no longer empathy.*

One does not simply feel; one must be seen feeling.

And in that shift, empathy is no longer about the other—it becomes about me.

The Media's Role in Performed Empathy

The world today is shaped by constant visibility. Everything is recorded, shared, and consumed. And so, even the most sacred human qualities—kindness, generosity, love—become subject to the same unconscious impulse: Show it. Validate it. Make it known.

The mind, conditioned by this environment, begins to measure its own emotions in the same way.

The question is no longer: Am I present?

Instead, it becomes: Does my presence look like presence?

Empathy cannot be seen. If it must be displayed, it is no longer empathy—it is identity. And identity always seeks an audience.

A deeply compassionate act may go unseen. A moment of genuine presence may leave no trace. And yet, in the world of the mind, what is unseen often feels as though it does not exist.

> *The moment you stop needing to be seen as compassionate, you finally are.*

So the impulse arises to prove it. To show others that we feel. But true empathy does not require witnesses. It does not need to be shared to be real.

It simply is.

The Compassion Illusion: When Caring Becomes a Role, Not a Reality

In the mind's search for significance, even empathy can become a form of competition.

Who grieves the loudest?

Who expresses the most outrage?

Who cares the most visibly?

And yet, true compassion is not found in intensity. It is not measured in volume. It is found in stillness, in presence, in the space where the mind no longer seeks to prove itself.

A quiet moment of listening carries more depth than a thousand public declarations. A single act of kindness, done without the need for recognition, holds more power than any display of concern.

The ego, however, does not recognize this. It seeks affirmation, not depth. It believes that to be compassionate, one must appear compassionate. That to care, one must be seen caring.

And so, empathy becomes performance.

The Illusion of Virtue in Visibility

During the *Black Lives Matter* protests of 2020, social media was flooded with black squares—symbols of solidarity posted by millions. And yet, for many, these gestures were the extent of their participation.

A moment of recognition, a display of awareness, and then—silence.

Was this empathy? Or was it the appearance of empathy?

The mind, caught in identification, often mistakes visibility for virtue.

But virtue is not found in what is seen. It is found in what is done, in the quiet choices that require no validation. Empathy, in its truest form, is invisible. It does not announce itself. It does not demand recognition. It does not require an audience. If it does, it is no longer empathy.

It is something else.

A Return to True Witnessing

The greatest act of empathy is presence. To be with suffering without needing to make it about oneself.

To feel without broadcasting.

To care without seeking acknowledgment.

To love without needing to be seen loving.

The deepest acts of love are invisible. True empathy does not announce itself. It simply exists.

It simply feels.

> Empathy does not need an audience. If it does, it is no longer empathy.

True empathy is effortless. It arises when the mind is still. It is not something to perform. It is something to allow.

When you are fully present, when you no longer need to be seen, you return to the essence of empathy. And in that stillness, in that quiet space where nothing needs to be proven—there, true connection begins.

Self-Reflection: Can I allow myself to feel without the need to be seen feeling? Am I moved to act by presence, or by the need for validation? Can I let go of the need to prove my compassion?

Forced Compassion: When Empathy Controls Instead of Connects

Can empathy be used as a tool of control? When compassion is forced, policed, or expected, it ceases to be a bridge between people—it becomes a means of enforcement.

Compassion does not control. Love does not force. Empathy does not demand to be seen. It is the silent presence that heals. The moment it must be proven, it is no longer empathy—it is control. It simply is—an open presence, a willingness to hold space for another's experience without making it one's own.

But when the mind takes hold of empathy, when it becomes a function of the ego rather than an expression of presence, it is no longer empathy. It is something else.

It becomes control.

This is how empathy is weaponized—not as a means of connection, but as a means of enforcing conformity, of dictating which emotions are correct, which responses are acceptable.

When empathy is no longer organic, but something that must be displayed, something that must be performed, it ceases to be a bridge between people. It becomes a tool of coercion.

Performative Empathy as a Tool for Social Power

The moment empathy becomes an expectation rather than a spontaneous arising of presence, it is no longer an act of love but an act of self-affirmation. It is no longer about being with another in their suffering. It is about being seen caring.

This is why displays of public concern are so often empty gestures. The mind, caught in its identification with morality, believes that in order to be compassionate, it must demonstrate compassion. It must prove itself.

And so, compassion becomes something external—a statement, a post, an expression meant to signal to the world: I feel the right things.

But real compassion needs no audience.

Corporate brands declare solidarity with causes while continuing exploitative practices. Public figures display concern, not because they truly care, but because their image depends on it. The external form of empathy is present, but the inner substance is absent.

Consider the case of H&M. In 2020, the fashion brand issued a public statement in support of Black Lives Matter. And yet, behind the scenes, the same company was profiting from exploitative labor conditions in developing nations.[1]

The illusion of empathy was there, but the reality was not. This is the nature of performative empathy—it seeks not to help, but to maintain an image. The ego does not care about true change. It cares about appearing virtuous.

And so, empathy is no longer about the other. It becomes about me.

Cancel Culture and the Policing of Empathy

The demand for performative empathy has created a culture in which emotions are policed. Not only must one hold the right beliefs, but one must feel in the right way.

---

[1] *Business Insider,* 2020

And if they do not—if their grief is not visible enough, if their outrage is not sufficient—they are shamed.

This is the nature of cancel culture. It is not simply about accountability. It is about emotional conformity.

The demand is not just for an apology. The demand is for proof—proof of suffering, proof of guilt, proof of emotional devastation. It is no longer enough to acknowledge wrongdoing. One must perform regret.

In 2021, pop star Billie Eilish faced backlash after an old video surfaced of her mouthing the words to a racial slur in a song. An apology was issued, but it was not enough. Critics demanded visible remorse, a display of suffering, a public act of self-flagellation to prove sincerity.[2]

This is not empathy. This is enforcement.

Genuine empathy does not dictate how another should feel. It does not demand suffering as proof of virtue.

It allows. It accepts. It understands.

Empathy is not meant to wound. But when it is forced, demanded, or used to shame, it is no longer a bridge—it is a cage.

The Moral Trap of "Not Caring Enough"

There is an unspoken demand in modern culture:

- You must care about everything.

- You must feel deeply about every injustice.

- You must show that you care.

And if you do not? You are indifferent. You are complicit.

But the human mind was not designed for infinite empathy.

Decades ago, a person's emotional world was shaped by the suffering they encountered directly—the people in their lives, the experiences in their immediate world. Now, through social media, one is bombarded with suffering from every corner of the planet. Every hour. Every moment.

The mind, overwhelmed, does not become more compassionate. It becomes numb. This is what psychologists call *compassion collapse*—when exposure to too much suffering does not increase empathy, but diminishes it.[3]

---

[2] *BBC, 2021*
[3] *Slovic, 2007*

The more suffering one witnesses without resolution, the more powerless they feel.And powerlessness leads to detachment.

This is why moral exhaustion is so prevalent in modern culture.

The expectation to care about everything, all at once, creates a sense of perpetual inadequacy. One can never do enough. One can never feel enough.

The result?

Not more compassion, but burnout. Not more action, but apathy.

When caring becomes an obligation rather than a natural arising, it ceases to be real.

The Demand for Public Grief

Empathy, when pure, is quiet. It does not demand display. But today, grief must be shown. Outrage must be announced. Solidarity must be proven.

Consider the Ukraine-Russia war in 2022. As the conflict unfolded, social media users began criticizing those who failed to publicly post solidarity messages for Ukraine.

The implication was clear: if you did not display concern, you did not care.[4]

But is that true?

If one does not announce their empathy, does it mean it is absent? Or is true empathy found in the quiet act, the unseen choice, the presence that does not need validation?

A moment of stillness with a grieving friend carries more weight than a thousand public declarations. Yet, in a world driven by visibility, the unseen often feels as though it does not exist.

And so, the mind seeks to prove its goodness.

But goodness, when forced, is no longer goodness.

It is obligation.

And obligation is not love.

Reclaiming Empathy: Breaking Free
from the Need to Prove

What happens when empathy is no longer a reaction, but a choice? Empathy

---

[4] *The Washington Post, 2022*

does not need proof. The moment it must be seen, it is no longer about the other—it is about you. To reclaim empathy, let go of the need to be seen as good. The moment you stop proving, you start being.

To see suffering, without making it one's own. To care, without needing to be seen caring. To act, without needing recognition.

This is not indifference. This is presence.

True empathy is not forced. It is not policed. It does not require performance. It arises naturally when the mind is still, when the ego no longer seeks affirmation.

The world does not need more forced expressions of empathy.

It needs presence.

It needs real, quiet, genuine love. The kind that does not need to be witnessed.

The kind that simply is.

> *When empathy is forced, it is no longer empathy. It is control.*

Breaking Free from the Weaponization of Empathy

The mind seeks to hold on—to label, to categorize, to control. Even something as pure as empathy is turned into a concept, a performance, a measurement of one's moral worth. But true empathy is not of the mind. It is of presence.

To reclaim empathy, one must step beyond identification, beyond the need to be seen, beyond the illusion that suffering must be absorbed in order to be acknowledged.

> *When empathy is quiet, it is real. When it is demanded, it ceases to exist.*

Empathy, when free of the mind's interference, is simple. It does not ask for validation. It does not require spectacle. It does not serve the ego.

The path to true empathy is not in grasping, but in releasing.

Recognizing Performative Empathy

The ego seeks affirmation, even in kindness. It asks: How do I appear? rather than How can I serve?

This is the shift from presence to performance. The quiet, natural impulse of compassion is replaced by an outward display—an identity to be maintained, an image to be protected.

True empathy does not need to be witnessed. It does not need to be declared. To recognize performative empathy is to see when the mind has inserted itself into compassion—when an act of kindness is no longer about the other, but about oneself.

When empathy requires acknowledgment, it is no longer empathy. It is self-concern.

Rejecting Emotional Policing

There is a growing expectation that one must not only care, but care in the right way. One must show concern. One must display the correct emotions. One must prove their depth of feeling.

But genuine emotions cannot be forced. They arise naturally, or not at all. The moment empathy is demanded, it ceases to be real.

When others dictate how one should feel, they are not calling forth compassion. They are demanding compliance.

True empathy allows. It does not dictate. It does not insist.

> *True compassion does not seek validation—it simply exists, like stillness, like breath.*

To reject emotional policing is to free oneself from the expectation that all suffering must be reacted to in a specific way.

Some suffering calls for action. Some for silence. Some for nothing at all.

When presence is lost, empathy becomes obligation.

And obligation is not love.

Practicing Selective Engagement

The mind tells you that you must care about everything. That every injustice, every suffering, every tragedy must become yours. But the mind was not built to carry infinite burdens.

Engaging with every crisis, reacting to every moment of pain—this is not compassion. It is compulsion. And compulsion does not serve. It only exhausts.

You do not have to react to everything in order to be a moral person.

Self-Reflection: For the next 24 hours, observe how often you feel the need to prove your empathy. Can you let go of that impulse? Can you simply be?"

You do not have to suffer alongside others in order to acknowledge their suffering. The greatest acts of empathy often happen in the quiet, in the unseen moments, in the presence that does not ask for recognition.

To step out of the cycle of endless reaction is not indifference.

It is wisdom.

The Return to Presence

Empathy, when unburdened by the mind, is one of the deepest expressions of human connection. But when it is distorted, when it is turned into a performance, a requirement, a tool of coercion, it ceases to be empathy at all.

The question is not whether empathy is good or bad. The question is whether it is real.

To remain truly compassionate in an age of moral theatrics, one must learn to separate genuine care from conditioned obligation.

When empathy is free from performance, it no longer drains—it nourishes.

When empathy is free from validation, it no longer divides—it unites.

And when empathy is free from expectation, it no longer depletes—it simply is.

"Empathy is about finding echoes of another person in yourself."

— Mohsin Hamid

Outrage Addiction Insight:
The Paradox of Empathy

Empathy, in its true form, is presence. It exists without effort, without seeking, without expectation. But when it becomes a compulsion, when it is driven by the need to react, to prove, to be seen, it becomes something else entirely.

Moral outrage activates the brain's reward pathways, triggering a release of dopamine—the same neurochemicals responsible for pleasure, motivation, and reinforcement of addictive behaviors.[5]

This means that standing up for others—or appearing to—can provide a rush of gratification, a sense of purpose, a validation of self.

Over time, this neurological cycle reinforces repeated engagement in outrage-driven behavior, particularly when it is met with external validation—likes, shares, social praise.[6]

Empathy, instead of being an act of stillness, becomes a cycle of reaction. Instead of being a quiet presence, it becomes an external identity.

The mind, drawn to the reward, seeks more. But what is sought is never enough. Ironically, this compulsive cycle does not lead to deeper connection. It leads to exhaustion.

When empathy is constantly engaged for external validation, it ceases to be a natural response. It becomes a habit.

A habit that, over time, depletes the very capacity for true, heartfelt empathy.

To break free, one must recognize this pattern. One must step out of the compulsion to react.

One must return to presence.

∞∞∞∞

True empathy does not weigh you down—it sets you free. Suffering for others does not lighten their burden; it only steals your own peace. You do not save the drowning by drowning with them. You save them by standing, by being the stillness they can reach for."

True empathy is the absence of need. It does not need to be seen, shared, or rewarded. When empathy is still, it is real. When it is demanded, it ceases to exist

---

[5] *Rothschild & Keefer, 2017*
[6] *Waytz, Dungan, & Young, 2015*

Empathy, when free from performance, is the deepest form of love. It does not seek validation. It does not demand recognition. It simply exists—like stillness, like breath, like the quiet presence of a friend who needs no words to be felt."

Self-Reflection: Each time you witness suffering, ask yourself: Am I truly here, or am I making this about me? See what happens when you let presence replace performance.

The Empathy Illusion

Empathy is often seen as an unquestioned good, yet there is a point where it ceases to serve connection and becomes an illusion—something we wear rather than something we feel.

This is the Empathy Illusion: when the act of caring becomes more about being seen as compassionate than about the compassion itself. When empathy becomes an identity rather than a response, it is no longer real.

> True empathy is not something you do—it is something you are. And when you no longer need to prove it, you finally become it.

Outrage Addiction Insight

Why does standing up for others sometimes feel addictive?

Research indicates that moral outrage activates the brain's reward system, releasing dopamine that reinforces feelings of moral superiority.[1] This neural reward creates a sense of validation and righteousness, encouraging repeated engagement in outrage-driven behavior—even when the empathy behind the outrage becomes superficial or self-serving.[2]

---

[1] *Rothschild & Keefer, 2017*
[2] *Waytz, Dungan, & Young, 2015*

Chapter Four

The Echo Chambers of Modern Discourse

"We don't see things as they are, we see them as we are."

— Anaïs Nin

The Rise of Information Echo Chambers

Information is no longer freely explored; it is curated and controlled. The digital landscape does not foster open inquiry—it thrives on confinement. What you see is not what is true but what is most profitable to show you.

> *The mind seeks certainty, but certainty is an illusion. To awaken is to see beyond the mind's conditioning.*

Modern discourse is no longer an open exchange of ideas. It has become a hall of mirrors, reflecting back only what one already believes. Rather than being challenged by new perspectives, people now exist in self-reinforcing thought loops, consuming information not to expand their awareness but to confirm their pre-existing identity.

What does this mean for human consciousness? It means that many no longer see reality as it is but as they wish it to be. They become lost in thought constructs—mental projections of the world that do not reflect the world itself.

Self-Reflection: Pause. Breathe. Observe your own mind. What are you clinging to? What is real beyond thought?

The Modern Landscape of Information Consumption

There was a time when information flowed through shared channels. People read the same newspapers, watched the same broadcasts, and engaged with diverse perspectives, even if they disagreed. There was a sense of common reality—an imperfect but collective foundation from which discourse emerged.

But today, the mind no longer seeks reality; it seeks validation. Algorithms, designed to maximize engagement, do not show people what is true but what will keep them watching, clicking, and reacting. Each interaction reinforces the illusion that one's worldview is complete, unchallenged, unshakable. And so, the world outside disappears, and what remains is a carefully curated narrative designed not to inform but to maintain the mental conditioning of the observer.

This is not accidental. Social media platforms have built engagement-driven algorithms that prioritize content that provokes the strongest emotions—particularly outrage.[1] The more anger, the more engagement. The more engagement, the more the system feeds the same thoughts back to the user, reinforcing a singular, narrow perspective. A self-created prison of the mind.

The Comfort of Echo Chambers

Platforms are not neutral spaces for discussion; they are engagement machines. The more polarized users become, the longer they stay. And the longer they stay, the more profit is extracted from their attention.

Social platforms ensure that users are fed content that aligns with their existing views, minimizing exposure to contradictory perspectives. Over time, this creates the illusion that one's perspective is not just valid but universally true.

Notice the mind's reaction. Does resistance arise? Dismissal? A need to refute? This is not truth—it is conditioning. It is confirmation bias.[2]

But beyond psychology, this is simply attachment to thought. The person identifies with their beliefs so deeply that questioning those beliefs feels like a threat to their very existence.

Yet all thought is conditioned. The way one perceives reality is shaped by

---

[1] *Tufekci, 2015*
[2] *Festinger, 1957*

experience, culture, and personal history. When the mind confuses thought for truth, it becomes trapped—defending illusions rather than seeking understanding.

Self-Reflection: *Pause. Feel the pull to defend what you believe. What if you let that go? What is left?*

The Danger of Homogenized Thought

What happens when an entire society becomes lost in echo chambers? It becomes fragmented. Dialogue is replaced by conflict. Disagreement is seen as an attack. Nuance is lost.

When exposure to diverse perspectives is minimized, intellectual growth is stunted. The algorithm does not serve truth—it serves reaction. The more you react, the more it feeds you the same emotions. Do you see the cycle? Step back. Do not follow it.

Homogenized thought is the enemy of presence. When the mind is full of conditioned narratives, it cannot be still. It cannot observe without immediately reacting. It cannot listen without preparing a response. It cannot see another human being beyond the mental labels it has already assigned to them.

This is how outrage thrives. The more people isolate themselves within ideological bubbles, the more reactive they become. The more reactive they become, the more they are controlled—not by truth, but by their own conditioned responses.

The world is not lacking intelligence. It is lacking awareness. The ability to step outside one's echo chamber, to observe one's own conditioned mind without becoming attached to its stories, is the beginning of true understanding.

"Your assumptions are your windows on the world. Scrub them off every once in a while, or the light won't come in." — Isaac Asimov

Breaking Free from the Echo Chamber

How does one escape this cycle? Not by replacing one belief system with another but by seeing the mind's conditioning for what it is. By realizing that every thought—no matter how strongly held—is ultimately just a thought.

Observe the mind's attachment to certainty.

Recognize how information is curated. Now pause. Feel the pull to react. Where is it coming from? Who benefits from your reaction? What if you did not engage? Actively seek out sources outside of algorithmic recommendations.

Engage with silence.

Step away from the constant stream of mental input. Observe the mind without feeding it more content.

In silence, clarity arises. Without external reinforcement, conditioned narratives begin to dissolve.

See beyond labels.

No person is simply 'right' or 'wrong.' Reality is not bound by the mind's categories.

The ability to listen—not just to respond, but to truly understand—creates space for deeper awareness.

∞∞∞∞

The modern mind is addicted to certainty, but certainty is an illusion. Echo chambers do not provide truth; they provide comfort. Yet, comfort is not the same as freedom.

To awaken is to see beyond the mind's conditioning—to recognize that every belief, every opinion, every reaction is a product of thought. Only by stepping outside these thought-constructs can one begin to engage with reality as it truly is.

Only then does awareness replace ideology. Only then does presence replace reaction. Only then is one truly free.

How Algorithms Shape What You See

There is a space between stimulus and reaction—a moment of stillness where true awareness exists. Yet, for many, this space has disappeared. In its place, there is only instant reactivity, a constant cycle of emotional provocation. The mind no longer observes reality; it consumes a version of reality shaped by algorithms.

You may believe that you are freely choosing the information you engage with. But is this true? Or is the information choosing you?

Social media is not a window to the world—it is a mirror, reflecting back only what will keep you engaged. And what captures attention best? Outrage. Fear. Division.

Every reaction feeds the system. Every moment of outrage is data. The more you engage, the more the algorithm pulls you deeper—not toward truth, but toward reaction.

Self-Reflection: Pause before you react. What if you simply watched the impulse—without acting on it? Try it now. See how the mind wants to pull you in.

> *You do not choose the information you see. The information chooses you.*

The Algorithmic Design of Modern Platforms

Algorithms do not seek truth. They do not ask, "What does this person need for deeper understanding?" Instead, they ask, "What will make this person stay?"

Facebook, Twitter, YouTube, and countless other platforms rely on engagement-driven models—systems that prioritize content that generates the strongest emotional responses.[3] A neutral, nuanced discussion does not trigger this response. But anger does. Fear does. The feeling of being "right" in the face of perceived ignorance does.

This is why outrage is not an accident of social media—it is its fuel. The longer you remain in a heightened state of reaction, the longer you stay on the platform. The longer you stay, the more data is collected, the more ads are shown, and the more profitable your attention becomes.

Outrage is a product. And you are the buyer.

Content evoking moral outrage spreads significantly faster and further than neutral content.[4] The angrier the post, the more engagement it receives. The more engagement it receives, the more similar content is recommended. And so, an individual scrolling through their feed is not exploring ideas—they are being guided, step by step, into a more extreme version of their existing beliefs.

The illusion is that one is merely "keeping up with the news." The reality is that one is being conditioned to react rather than to reflect.

---

[3] *Tufekci, 2015*
[4] *Brady et al., 2017*

> *When outrage becomes habitual, it is no longer about truth—it is about the pleasure of reaction.*

The Psychology of Confirmation Bias

Why do people gravitate toward information that reinforces their beliefs rather than challenges them? The answer is not intellectual—it is emotional.

The human mind avoids discomfort. When confronted with a perspective that contradicts what it already believes, it experiences cognitive dissonance—a state of mental tension that demands resolution.[5] The easiest resolution is not to examine the conflicting idea but to reject it outright.

This is why social media platforms become echo chambers. Individuals do not merely encounter information—they curate it. They unfollow those who challenge them, mute those who introduce doubt, and engage only with those who confirm their perspective. This is not a conscious deception but an unconscious protection of the ego—the part of the mind that clings to identity, to certainty, to the feeling of being "right."

This is also why agreement is pleasurable. When you hear something that aligns with what you already believe, notice the small sense of pleasure that arises. This is not truth—it is conditioning. It is the mind rewarding itself for being 'right.' The more you seek this reward, the harder it becomes to see beyond it.[6]

The mind enjoys agreement. It resists contradiction. And in this resistance, it mistakes familiarity for truth. This is why people do not merely disagree in modern discourse—they react with disgust, anger, and a deep sense of personal violation. It is not just about ideas—it is about identity.

The more users engage with algorithmically favored perspectives, the more those views are amplified, creating a curated version of reality that deepens ideological entrenchment.

Self-Reflection: Look at your own screen. Every headline, every post—is it showing you the world? Or is it showing you what will make you react?

See the pattern. Step outside it.

---

[5] *Festinger, 1957*

[6] *Sharot et al., 2016*

The Escalation of Outrage Through Selective Exposure

Once a person is inside an information bubble, the intensity of their reactions must increase to sustain engagement. A moderate level of outrage is not enough—each subsequent exposure must feel more urgent, more extreme, more personal.

Consider how a single event is reshaped by different ideological media landscapes. The same set of facts is interpreted in wildly different ways, shaped by the needs of the audience. The goal is not to inform—it is to escalate emotion.

Research on media consumption patterns has shown that people who engage primarily with partisan news sources become more extreme in their views over time.[7] The more they consume, the less they tolerate dissent. The less they tolerate dissent, the deeper they fall into ideological entrenchment.

This is how outrage becomes habitual. The mind, conditioned by repetition, begins to seek out things to be offended by. It scans for violations, for injustices, for anything that can justify another dopamine rush of moral superiority.

Moral outrage expressed online is not just a reaction—it is a learned behavior. The more one participates in outrage-driven discussions, the more habitual the behavior becomes. The more habitual it becomes, the harder it is to disengage.[8]

This is why many people feel trapped in a cycle of emotional reactivity. They are not choosing their outrage. Their outrage is choosing them.

> *If your beliefs were suddenly proven wrong, who would you be?*

Breaking the Cycle of Algorithmic Conditioning

How does one escape an information bubble? Not by replacing it with another, but by seeing it for what it is—a construct, a mental framework that distorts reality rather than revealing it.

Pause before reacting.
Notice when the mind instantly resists an opposing viewpoint.

Observe the reaction without acting on it. Is it discomfort? Anger? Fear?

Simply becoming aware of the reaction weakens its control.

---

[7] *Bail et al., 2018*
[8] *Crockett, 2017*

Expose yourself to disconfirming perspectives.

Seek out long-form discussions, not just headlines.

Read arguments without the need to agree or disagree.

Observe how quickly the mind tries to reject opposing views.

Step away from the feed.

Silence is the enemy of outrage. Without constant input, the mind settles.

Ask: Who am I without these narratives? What exists beyond these conditioned thoughts?

∘∘∘∘∘

The mind is restless. It seeks reaction, not truth. It is fed not what will enlighten it but what will entrench it. And yet, one can step outside this cycle. One can see the game being played and refuse to participate.

To awaken is to see not just the information one consumes but the mechanism that delivers it. It is to recognize that what appears to be reality is only a fragment carefully selected to reinforce the self.

Truth is not found in the endless stream of mental noise. Truth is found in the space between reactions, in the willingness to step beyond one's own conditioned identity, in the ability to observe without judgment and to think without attachment.

Step back. Watch the mind react. But do not follow it.

In that stillness, you are free.

The Outrage Loop: Why Reactivity Feeds Itself

There is a moment—a brief, almost imperceptible moment—before reaction takes hold. A space of stillness where one could choose not to be pulled into the current. But for many, this space has been lost. The reaction comes automatically, forcefully, as though it has a life of its own.

This is the nature of outrage. It does not arise in isolation. It feeds on itself, growing stronger with each reaction, each validation, each escalation. It does not dissolve—it demands more.

Yet, what is it that is being fed? Is it truth? Or is it simply a pattern, a cycle of conditioned response?

The Cycle of Emotional Reactivity

Every time a user reacts with outrage, the platform registers this as engagement and pushes similar content, reinforcing reactionary thinking. Over time, this process reshapes public discourse, prioritizing emotional intensity over intellectual depth.

The world of social media and digital platforms functions as an extension of this. It does not offer you an open landscape of ideas. Instead, it provides a mirror, reflecting back what will trigger the strongest response.

Outrage is not a byproduct—it is the business model. Every conflict fuels engagement. Every engagement feeds the algorithm. The system does not care what you believe, only that you keep believing harder.

A person in this cycle may believe they are engaging with reality. But in truth, they are engaged in a feedback loop of their own conditioned mind. And because reaction feels instantaneous, it is mistaken for truth.

What would happen if you simply did not react? Not as suppression but as observation. If you allowed the emotion to arise but did not feed it? This is where true awareness begins.

Dopamine-Driven Validation

The more outrage is expressed, the more it is rewarded. But what exactly is being rewarded? Truth? Insight? Or simply the act of reaction itself?

The mind mistakes outrage for purpose. Each time you react, dopamine rewards the illusion of moral clarity. But this is not awareness—it is compulsion.[9] This means that each time one engages in an outrage-driven conversation, a small reward is given. A like. A comment. A sense of agreement from others.

It feels good, even if only momentarily. The self feels affirmed, seen, and justified. But this feeling is fleeting. It does not last, so more outrage must be sought, more validation chased.

This is why online outrage does not remain at the same intensity—it must increase. The mind quickly adapts to what once felt satisfying. What was shocking yesterday is ordinary today. So, the reaction must become stronger, the language more extreme, and the accusations more forceful.

It does not stop. It only seeks more. More reaction. More certainty. More

---

[9] *Rothschild & Keefer, 2017*

outrage. More emptiness. To break this cycle is to step back and see it for what it is: a habit, not an identity. A pattern, not a truth.

The Spiral Effect: Escalating Outrage for Visibility

The more one engages in this cycle, the harder it is to stop. Why? Because outrage, like all habitual thoughts, seeks reinforcement.

Consider a crowded space where everyone is speaking. To be heard, one must speak louder. If a person whispers, they will be ignored. So, the voice rises. The words become sharper. The statements more aggressive. Until soon, communication is no longer about dialogue—it is about volume.

This is what happens in digital outrage. Over time, a simple disagreement is no longer enough. To gain attention and to receive validation, one must escalate.

A study found that exposure to outrage-driven content increases political and ideological extremism over time, not necessarily because beliefs are shifting but because the intensity of reaction must increase to maintain engagement.[10]

In this way, outrage does not just sustain itself—it amplifies. It becomes louder, angrier, less reflective. The goal is no longer understanding. The goal is winning.

But winning what? And at what cost?

Stepping Out of the Loop

A person caught in this cycle may believe they have no choice. That outrage is the necessary response. That reactivity is a sign of awareness. But awareness does not exist within the reaction—it exists in the space before it.

To step out of this loop does not mean to suppress outrage. It means to witness it without becoming it.

Notice the impulse to react.

Feel the pull of reaction as it arises.

Do not act on it immediately. Simply observe it.

Recognize the cycle.

When a thought triggers outrage, ask:Is this response to truth or to habit?

If you were not rewarded for this reaction, would you still have it?

Allow stillness.

---

[10] *Bail et al., 2018*

Step away from digital platforms designed to provoke reaction.

Observe how the mind seeks stimulation through outrage—and notice what exists beyond it.

∞∞∞∞

The mind believes it must react. Must fight. Must be right. But what if it didn't?

Watch the reaction arise.

And let it pass—like a cloud drifting across the sky

In that moment, you step outside of the loop. You are no longer being fed outrage. You are no longer fueling it in return.

Instead, you are free.

Self-Reflection: Before moving on, stop. Notice—how does your mind feel right now? Stagnant? Defensive? Curious? These are just thoughts. Observe them. But do not follow them.

The Social Cost of Divided Minds

When thought becomes confined, so does the world. The more rigidly the mind clings to its constructed reality, the more it resists anything that challenges it. This is the nature of the echo chamber—not a space of shared wisdom but a self-reinforcing enclosure where truth becomes secondary to the comfort of certainty. In such a space, dissent is not tolerated, nuance is unwelcome, and the ability to think beyond conditioned responses begins to atrophy.

What happens when an entire society moves in this direction? The cost is not just personal—it is collective. When questioning is punished, truth is no longer discovered—it is dictated.

The Erosion of Intellectual Diversity

Creativity, insight, and human progress arise from the meeting of different ideas, from the friction of opposing viewpoints that force a deeper contemplation. Without this, thought does not evolve—it stagnates.

Echo chambers, by design, suppress dissenting voices. They do not simply reinforce dominant narratives; they actively filter out perspectives that might disrupt the prevailing ideology.[11] The result is not the expansion of knowledge but its narrowing.

In an environment where ideological purity is demanded, thinkers, artists, and scholars begin to self-censor. Not because they no longer have ideas but because the risk of voicing them has become too high.

A survey by the Foundation for Individual Rights and Expression (FIRE) found that over 60% of university students in the U.S. hesitate to express views they believe are unpopular.[12] The same pattern emerges in workplaces, social settings, and even within families. When the cost of disagreement is ostracization, silence becomes self-preservation.

But silence is also the death of inquiry. A society that discourages challenge does not strengthen truth—it weakens it.

The Rise of Tribal Identity

The need to belong is fundamental. From the earliest human societies, survival depended on inclusion within a group. To be cast out was to be left vulnerable.

This same primal instinct still operates today but in a different form. A divided public is not a failure of the system—it is its greatest success. Polarization keeps people engaged. It keeps them predictable. And above all, it keeps them distracted.

Studies on social identity theory demonstrate that group affiliation is not just about shared beliefs but about emotional reinforcement.[13] In modern echo chambers, outrage becomes the currency of belonging. Every reaction feeds the system. Each moment of outrage is stored, analyzed, and used to shape future content, keeping users locked in an emotional loop.

This is why online discourse so often escalates—not because people are genuinely seeking resolution, but because demonstrating outrage solidifies their position within the group. Polarization is not an accident; it is an asset. The deeper the division, the more predictable—and profitable—public behavior becomes.

Now, the mind is not just conditioned—it is policed.

What happens when identity is built entirely on opposition? When loyalty to a group is based not on shared purpose but on shared hostility? The result is not unity but perpetual division.

---

[11] *Sunstein, 2017*
[12] *FIRE, 2022*
[13] *Tajfel & Turner, 1979*

A society where people define themselves by what they are against rather than what they stand for is a society in conflict with itself.

The Fear of Speaking Out

Perhaps the most insidious consequence of echo chambers is not what is said but what is left unsaid.

Fear is the silent enforcer of ideological conformity. It does not need explicit rules; it operates through unspoken consequences. If someone witnesses a colleague being "called out" for an opinion, they learn the lesson: do not step out of line. If a writer sees another writer being denounced for questioning a narrative, they understand: certain ideas are untouchable.

This creates a culture of preemptive self-censorship, where individuals regulate their own thoughts before they are even spoken. Not because they lack conviction but because the cost of honesty has become too great.

A report by the Cato Institute (2020) found that 62% of Americans feel they cannot openly express their political views for fear of professional or social consequences. This is not a theoretical issue. It is a measurable shift in how people engage with truth.

When fear governs discourse, the result is intellectual paralysis. And in that paralysis, real problems go unaddressed, real injustices remain unchallenged, and real progress halts.

Breaking Free from Collective Fear

The way forward is not found in louder voices or greater polarization. It is found in the courage to step outside of conditioned narratives and into a space of open awareness.

Recognize the fear.
Notice the moments when you hesitate to speak.

Ask: Is my silence coming from wisdom or from fear of rejection?

Engage without attachment.
Read opposing perspectives—not to argue, but to observe.

Notice when your mind reacts defensively. What is it protecting?

Detach identity from ideology.
Understand that your beliefs are not you.

If an idea changes, does your sense of self dissolve? If so, was it ever real?

Create space for difficult conversations.

Instead of fearing disagreement, welcome it.

Recognize that being "right" is not the goal—awakening to deeper understanding is.

∞∞∞

A mind trapped in an echo chamber does not see itself as confined. It believes it is standing in truth simply because it hears nothing else.

But truth is not found in certainty. It is found in openness. The willingness to step beyond the known, beyond the comfortable, beyond the conditioned mind.

When a person chooses to listen without the need to defend, to speak without the fear of consequence, to engage without the illusion of identity—then the echo chamber collapses.

You are not your reactions. You are not your outrage. When you step beyond conditioned thought, you see clearly. You think freely. And in that space, you reclaim your mind.

But awareness.

Cultural Silos: Why Debate Is Dying

There was a time when discourse was an exchange—when words were meant to connect rather than divide. A time when opposing viewpoints could exist in the same space without hostility, without the desperate need for one to dominate the other. But now, conversation has fractured into parallel realities, each reinforcing itself, each rejecting all that lies beyond its borders.

This is what happens when dialogue is replaced by monologue, when discussion becomes performance, and when silence is safer than honesty. The mind retreats into the illusion of certainty, and the world grows smaller.

The Fragmentation of Public Discourse

Modern discourse is no longer a shared experience—it is a series of disconnected narratives, each speaking only to those who already agree. This is not debate; it is insulation.

Social media was once thought to be the great unifier, a space where voices from all perspectives could be heard. Instead, it has become a labyrinth of self-reinforcing ideas, where algorithms ensure that opposing viewpoints do not cross paths unless framed as threats.[14]

Exposure to opposing views should broaden the mind. Instead, it hardens it. Studies show that when confronted with contradiction, people double down on their beliefs, not question them. The result? Polarization deepens. Bail et al. (2018)

What does this tell us? That the fragmentation of public discourse is not accidental. It is the result of a deep attachment to identity, where viewpoints are no longer seen as ideas but as extensions of the self.

When an idea is challenged, the person feels challenged. And when one's identity is at stake, debate is no longer about understanding—it is about survival.

This is why conversation has become war.

Polarization Through Isolation

Imagine two islands. Each believes itself to be the entirety of the world. Each has its own rules, its own language, its own sacred truths. The idea that another island could exist—one with different customs and different truths—is not just unthinkable; it is offensive.

This is how ideological silos function. They do not simply separate people—they create realities so insulated that encountering an opposing view feels like an attack.

In this state, disagreement is no longer an exchange—it is a moral failing. A person outside the accepted narrative is not simply wrong; they are dangerous, unworthy, and perhaps even inhuman.

Partisan animosity in the United States is higher than at any point in modern history, with members of both major political parties viewing the other side as dishonest, immoral, and a threat to society. [15]

This is not a disagreement over policies or principles. This is tribal warfare masked as moral clarity.

And the consequence? Not just polarization but the complete inability to engage with those outside one's ideological silo.

A conversation that might have once begun with curiosity—"Why do you believe that?"—is now replaced with dismissal, outrage, or condemnation.

---

[14] *Pariser, 201*
[15] *Pew Research, 2020*

> *A world that flattens into 'us vs. them' is a world that no longer listens.*

The Death of Nuance in Public Debate

Nuance is the first casualty of polarization. The second is reason.

Nuance requires space—the space to think, to reflect, to hold two truths at once. But outrage is impatient. It demands immediate certainty and immediate reaction. And so, complexity is discarded in favor of simplicity:

- If you do not fully agree, you are an enemy.

- If you express doubt, you are a traitor.

- If you listen to the other side, you are complicit.

As political polarization increases, people become less likely to trust media sources that challenge their beliefs, opting instead for outlets that reinforce their worldview.[16] The result? A world that flattens into binary thinking—right vs. wrong, us vs. them.

But reality is not binary. Truth does not exist in absolutes. And when we insist that it does, we shrink human existence into a caricature of good and evil.

This is why debate feels impossible now. Because for many, there is no debate. There is only victory or defeat.

And so, the mind closes further. The world narrows. The walls of the ideological silo become thicker, stronger, more impenetrable.

And in the silence of what was once a shared public discourse, something essential is lost.

> *To step outside the echo chamber does not mean to agree. It means to listen.*

Breaking Free from the Illusion of Division

The way forward is not to demand agreement. It is to see the illusion for what it is—a construct of the mind, reinforced by a system that profits from division.

Question Your Triggers.

---

[16] *Levendusky, 2013*

When disagreement arises, pause.

Are you defending truth—or defending identity?

Engage with difference, not as threat, but as opportunity.

Read a perspective you normally reject—not to argue, but to observe.

Practice listening without immediately forming a counterpoint.

Step outside of ideological identity.

If your beliefs were suddenly proven wrong, who would you be?

Realize that identity attached to ideology is not identity—it is attachment to thought.

Hold space for nuance.

Not everything is absolute. Not everything is simple.

Truth is often found in contradiction, in paradox, in the willingness to say: I do not have to be right. I have to be open.

ooooo

The walls of the ideological silo are not real. They exist only in the mind.

But a mind that clings to certainty cannot see beyond them. A mind that fears contradiction will never know freedom.

The moment you step outside of certainty, you step into awareness.

And in awareness, debate is no longer a battle—it is a doorway.

Outrage Addiction Insight: How Echo Chambers Hook You

Why does outrage thrive in echo chambers? The answer lies in the way modern digital platforms are designed to reward emotional intensity over reasoned discourse. Social media algorithms do not exist to broaden perspectives—they exist to maximize engagement. And nothing drives engagement quite like outrage.

Every time a user reacts angrily to a piece of content, the algorithm registers that as a sign of deep interest and serves up more of the same. This creates a loop where users are constantly exposed to increasingly inflammatory content that reinforces their pre-existing beliefs.[17]

---

[17] *Pariser, 2011*

The dopamine-fueled validation that comes from outrage engagement—likes, shares, retweets—acts as a psychological reward, reinforcing the cycle.[18] Over time, individuals become trapped in an ecosystem where their outrage is not just a reaction but a conditioned response.

This is why stepping outside an ideological bubble feels uncomfortable—it disrupts the neural feedback loop that has been trained to seek reinforcement rather than challenge. The cycle continues not because people seek truth but because they seek confirmation.

Without awareness, the mind remains caught in this perpetual loop of outrage, validation, and escalation, mistaking it for meaningful discourse. But awareness creates choice. And choice is the first step toward breaking free.

"The greatest enemy of knowledge is not ignorance, it is the illusion of knowledge."
— *Stephen Hawking*

Outrage Addiction Insight

Why does surrounding yourself with like-minded opinions feel so satisfying?

Studies reveal that confirmation bias activates the brain's reward circuitry, releasing dopamine when beliefs are reaffirmed.[1] This neurological feedback loop makes echo chambers psychologically addictive, as exposure to agreeable ideas produces feelings of comfort and intellectual validation.[2]

---

[1] Nickerson, 1998
[2] Sharot, Korn, & Dolan, 2011

---

[18] Tufekci, 2015

Chapter Five

The Media's Role in Outrage Culture

"The media's the most powerful entity on earth. They have the power to make the innocent guilty and to make the guilty innocent."
— *Malcolm X*

Outrage Sells

The mind, wired for instant reaction, gravitates toward the loudest, most provocative narratives. News is no longer a reflection of reality—it's a carefully engineered emotional stimulant.

Outrage is not incidental to this model—it is the model. The more reactive the audience, the more profitable the content. This is why media companies are not merely reporting on outrage, they are actively cultivating it.

> *Outrage is the business model. Without it, the media industry collapses.*

The Business Model of Modern Media

In the past, information was sought out when needed. A person would read the news, absorb what was relevant, and move on with their life. Now, information seeks out the individual—unceasing, aggressive, and emotionally charged.

Every headline, every notification, every breaking news alert is designed not to inform, but to demand reaction. The longer a person stays emotionally engaged, the more clicks, shares, and revenue the platform generates.[1] Outrage ensures that attention does not waver. It keeps the mind gripped, reactive, and perpetually dissatisfied.

A study analyzing digital engagement found that negative, emotionally charged content spreads significantly faster than neutral or positive content.[2] This is not accidental—it is the deliberate exploitation of human psychology.

The media doesn't sell news—it sells your outrage. This cycle fuels engagement, drives ad revenue, and keeps audiences in a constant state of reactivity. Awareness is the first step to breaking free.

The Shift from Information to Sensationalism

News organizations once acted as gatekeepers of truth, seeking to provide balanced, well-researched perspectives. That function has been displaced by a race for engagement, where the most extreme interpretations of reality gain the most traction.

The shift was gradual. As newspapers struggled to maintain readership in the digital era, they discovered that conflict, fear, and outrage drove higher engagement than objective reporting. Social media only accelerated the trend. News that provoked anger or disgust generated far more shares and interactions than factual reporting.[3]

Where there is no immediate controversy, one is manufactured. Headlines are crafted to elicit an emotional reaction before the article is even read. News cycles focus less on relaying events and more on framing them in a way that fuels continued outrage. The question is no longer, What happened? but Who is to blame?

This is how discourse has been reduced to perpetual hostility—a world where every event is an opportunity to provoke, divide, and monetize emotional reactivity.

The Emotional Manipulation of Viewers

The effect of this constant stream of outrage is a gradual erosion of inner stillness. The present moment is no longer enough. One must always be watching, reacting, and choosing sides.

---

[1] *Hindman, 2018*
[2] *Berger & Milkman, 2012.*
[3] *Vosoughi, Roy, & Aral, 2018*

Media outlets understand this well. They do not present information as something to be contemplated, but as a crisis that demands immediate emotional engagement. Fear-based narratives activate the amygdala, the brain's fear-processing center, triggering a heightened sense of urgency.[4]

Once the nervous system is conditioned to respond, disengagement becomes difficult. The mind seeks out the very thing that keeps it agitated, believing that the next update, the next headline, will resolve the unease. But it never does. The cycle sustains itself indefinitely.

The individual becomes trapped—not by external forces, but by their own conditioned need to react. The more outrage one consumes, the more the mind craves it.

> *Truth is quiet. Outrage is loud. The mind, conditioned for stimulation, follows the noise.*

But awareness creates a shift. One begins to see how this cycle functions, not as an inevitable reality, but as a game designed to keep the mind restless and divided. And in that awareness, the possibility of stepping away arises.

But why does this work so well? Why does outrage outperform reason, nuance, or even entertainment in the media economy? The answer lies in the psychology of fear—because a mind in fear is a mind that does not question

---

Self-Reflection: The more reactive I become, the more profitable I am to the system. How often do I consume media that fuels my emotions rather than informs me?

Sensationalism and Fear: Profiting from Outrage

"If it bleeds, it leads." — Traditional Journalism Adage

A mind conditioned by fear is a mind that is easily controlled. In an unconscious state, it does not question, it reacts. This is what media outlets have

---

[4] *Zillmann, 2000.*

learned to cultivate—not information, but emotion, not awareness, but reactivity. The news is no longer simply a reflection of events but a carefully engineered product designed to maximize emotional engagement.

Outrage is currency. Fear is leverage. The more deeply one is caught in this emotional pull, the harder it becomes to step back and observe.

The Economics of Sensationalism

Media corporations don't exist to inform—you do not pay for the news. Advertisers do. And in the digital era, survival isn't about truth, it's about engagement. Clicks. Outrage. Retention.[5]

In a digital economy where attention is the most valuable commodity, the most profitable content is not that which enlightens, but that which provokes. Each click, each comment, each share reinforces the system. The more emotional engagement a story generates, the more advertising dollars flow to the platform hosting it.[6]

Outrage outperforms neutrality. Sensationalism eclipses accuracy. The stories that spread are not necessarily the most truthful, but the most inflammatory.[7]

This is why headlines are crafted not to inform, but to trigger emotional responses. News cycles do not simply cover crises; they stretch them, magnify them, feed on them. Fear and indignation ensure that the audience keeps coming back—not for resolution, but for the next hit of anxiety.

And so, news becomes less about reality and more about the drama surrounding it. Less about what is, and more about what must be feared, fought, or condemned.

The Psychology of Fear and Outrage

Fear is a powerful force because it demands immediate attention. The brain is wired to prioritize threats over neutral information—a survival mechanism that once protected humans from physical danger but now leaves them vulnerable to a never-ending cycle of media-driven anxiety.[8]

Outrage operates in the same way. It creates an illusion of urgency, making

---

[5] *McChesney, 2015*
[6] *Hindman, 2018*
[7] *Vosoughi, Roy, & Aral, 2018*
[8] *Soroka, Fournier, & Nir, 2019*

every event feel like a crisis that requires immediate emotional investment. The more the mind is trained to react, the more it mistakes stimulation for importance.

When someone sees a breaking news alert filled with emotionally charged language, their amygdala—the brain's fear center—activates, triggering a physiological response of stress and vigilance.[9] The news then becomes not just information, but a stimulus that keeps the nervous system in a perpetual state of agitation.

Over time, this pattern conditions the mind to crave outrage as a form of stimulation. People begin seeking out content that reinforces their anxieties, not because it provides clarity, but because it feeds a learned dependence on heightened emotional states.[10]

To break free, one must first become aware of the cycle: the impulse to react, the compulsion to stay engaged, the belief that outrage is necessary. Awareness disrupts the pattern. Awareness reveals the manipulation behind the constant stimulation.

Self-Reflection: When I feel anger or outrage from a news story, do I pause and investigate, or do I immediately react and share?

> Outrage does not make you powerful—it makes you predictable. And in predictability, the system profits.

Media Tactics That Exploit Outrage

The mechanics of media-driven outrage are subtle, but deliberate. News organizations do not simply report; they frame, amplify, and repeat narratives designed to provoke emotional investment.

Fear-Mongering Headlines

Stories are framed as existential threats, even when the actual risk is minimal.

Headlines use words like crisis, disaster, catastrophe, unprecedented, ensuring an emotional response before any critical thought occurs.

---

[9] *Zillmann, 2000*
[10] *Tufekci, 2015*

Selective Framing to Amplify Controversy

Information is not presented in its full complexity but curated to fit a narrative.

Stories that provoke conflict are elevated, while those that promote understanding are buried.

What is omitted is often as significant as what is included.

Emotional Language Designed to Provoke Reactions

The language of journalism has shifted from factual reporting to opinion-laden descriptions that shape the reader's perception before they even process the content.

Stories are not just reported; they are loaded with implied moral judgment, conditioning the audience to react rather than reflect.

The way news is framed shapes how we perceive reality. Are you consuming information—or just reacting to engineered narratives?

Awareness as Liberation

The first step in breaking free from this cycle is to recognize the pattern. One must observe how information is presented, how the mind reacts, and how emotions are used as tools of manipulation.

Ask:

- Is this information or is it provocation?
- Does this story encourage understanding, or does it feed division?
- Am I reacting, or am I truly seeing?

The moment one becomes conscious of these tactics, their power begins to dissolve. Without unconscious reactivity, sensationalism loses its hold.

And in that space of awareness, the individual is no longer a consumer of outrage but an observer of it.

And in observation, there is freedom.

But if outrage is profitable, how much of it is real? What if offense itself is not an organic reaction, but a manufactured product—designed, amplified, and distributed for maximum engagement?

Manufacturing Offense: Media-Manipulated Outrage Cycles

The unconscious mind is easily led. It does not see events as they are but as they are framed. A person caught in the cycle of outrage does not question why they feel anger, only that they do. The reaction is automatic, conditioned, expected. But where does it come from? And who is cultivating it?

Outrage does not simply appear. It is manufactured, sustained, and monetized. The news is no longer an observation of reality but a machine that selects, amplifies, and distorts events to fit a predetermined narrative. Each day brings a fresh controversy, each one demanding immediate emotional investment before the last has even faded.

When offense is curated and outrage is encouraged, what remains is not truth, but a reality shaped by those who profit from division.

> *Outrage does not arise—it is placed. The question is, by whom?*

The Cycle of Manufactured Outrage – Outrage doesn't emerge naturally; it is deliberately cultivated through a predictable sequence of media manipulation. From identifying a minor incident to embedding it into collective memory, this cycle ensures that emotional reactivity remains high and engagement never wavers.

The Cycle of Manufactured Outrage

What begins as a single event—perhaps a statement taken out of context, a social media post from years ago, or a minor dispute—is elevated into a cultural flashpoint. The process unfolds in distinct, predictable stages:

1. **Identification:** A seemingly minor incident is chosen, not for its objective importance, but for its potential to trigger emotional engagement.

2. **Amplification:** News outlets, commentators, and influencers seize upon the story, framing it as an urgent moral crisis. Headlines become deliberately provocative, ensuring that the initial narrative takes hold before facts emerge.

3. **Outrage Mobilization:** Social media magnifies the controversy. Users share, comment, and react—often without investigating the full context.

4. Escalation: As more people engage, the story expands beyond its original scope. Opposing sides emerge, cementing ideological battle lines.

5. Normalization: The manufactured outrage becomes part of public discourse, feeding future cycles of controversy and division.

This is not organic discourse. It is engineered manipulation—designed to trap the mind in a never-ending cycle of reaction, anger, and exhaustion. A society conditioned to outrage is a society that cannot think clearly.

The role of the media is not to inform, but to incite. Not to clarify, but to stir confusion.

> *The more you react, the less you think. The angrier you get, the easier you are to control.*

Case Studies of Media-Driven Outrage

The speed with which an event becomes a "crisis" is remarkable, yet wholly predictable. There are countless examples, but a few illustrate how easily misinformation, selective reporting, and media framing can manipulate public emotion.

The Covington Catholic High School Incident (2019)

A brief video clip circulated online appeared to show a group of high school students mocking a Native American activist at the Lincoln Memorial. The story exploded, with headlines condemning the students as symbols of privileged hostility. The outrage was immediate, widespread, and absolute.

Then the full video emerged. The narrative was false. The confrontation had been misrepresented, and the students had been standing still while an activist approached them. By then, however, the damage was done. Careers were ruined, threats were made, and media organizations quietly retracted their original reports—but only after the outrage had served its purpose.[11]

The Jussie Smollett Hoax (2019)

When actor Jussie Smollett claimed he had been the victim of a hate crime in Chicago, the media immediately framed the event as a damning reflection of

---

[11] *McBride, 2020*

society's worst impulses. Major outlets amplified the story without skepticism, presenting Smollett as a martyr of intolerance.

When evidence later revealed that Smollett had staged the attack, there was no comparable media correction, no mass retraction of the narrative that had been force-fed to the public. The manufactured outrage had already served its role in reinforcing a predetermined worldview.[12]

Both cases illustrate the same cycle: a rush to moral outrage, a lack of initial scrutiny, and a quiet retreat once the outrage has been successfully monetized.

Self-Reflection: Have I ever been emotionally manipulated by a headline or a viral story, only to later discover the full context changed my perception?

The Role of Visual Media in Amplifying Emotional Reactions

A single image can override reason. The mind does not analyze—it reacts. It sees an expression, a moment frozen in time, and assumes it understands. But what the mind sees is often only what it has been primed to see.

The news industry understands this well. An article may present one version of a story, but the chosen photograph dictates how the reader will feel about it.

– A protest, framed at the right angle, can appear either peaceful or violent.

– A politician's mid-sentence facial expression can be used to suggest arrogance or compassion.

– A headline paired with an emotionally charged image can render the article's actual content irrelevant.

And then there is video—the most powerful tool in media manipulation. Carefully selected clips, stripped of context, leave no room for nuance or complexity. Viewers are presented not with truth, but with a version of reality designed to elicit maximum emotional reaction.[13]

The manufactured outrage, the media narratives, the images and videos—all function to bypass critical thought and anchor the viewer in a cycle of conditioned emotional response. The goal is not to inform, but to condition reactivity.

---

[12] *Sexton, 2021*
[13] *Rose, 2012*

To step outside this cycle is not to disengage from reality, but to reclaim one's own perception from those who seek to manipulate it.

Self-Reflection: Am I forming my opinions based on investigation or reaction?

Awareness as the Only Escape

The moment outrage is seen not as spontaneous, but as cultivated, its hold weakens. The mind, when conscious, no longer serves as a vessel for manipulation.

One begins to question:

- Why was this specific event chosen as a national crisis?
- What is omitted from this narrative?
- Who benefits from my emotional investment in this outrage?

The act of watching without immediate reaction breaks the cycle. In observation, the mind is no longer controlled, no longer gripped by unconscious emotional engagement. And in that space, there is freedom.

The Responsibility of Consumers: How We Feed the Machine

There is a fundamental truth that many overlook: outrage cannot exist without participation. The news does not shout into a void; it is received, absorbed, and acted upon. The cycle is only complete when the audience engages—clicking, sharing, reacting. Each interaction, each emotional response, sustains the very system that breeds division.

But does the consumer see this? Or does he believe himself to be a passive observer—merely absorbing the world as it is presented?

To recognize one's own role in fueling the outrage machine is to become conscious of the unconscious habits that perpetuate it. And with awareness, one is no longer controlled.

The Attention Economy: Why Your Clicks Matter

Modern media is no longer structured around truth but around engagement. The news must not merely inform—it must captivate, provoke, sustain attention. A neutral headline fades. A scandalous one thrives.

The consumer does not realize that his attention is the product being sold. News organizations, social media platforms, and digital advertisers do not profit from facts—they profit from clicks, views, and shares. The more a story inflames, shocks, or outrages, the more valuable it becomes.

This is why news outlets amplify fear, division, and controversy. Sensationalism is not a byproduct of modern journalism—it is the business model itself.

> *In the digital economy, your attention is the product. Every click, every reaction—sold to the highest bidder.*

The Psychological Cost of Constant Engagement

To engage with outrage is to invite its energy into oneself. The body does not distinguish between real and perceived threats; it simply reacts. Every moment spent immersed in the media's theater of crisis keeps the nervous system in a state of heightened reactivity.

- The heart races in response to a provocative headline.
- The mind fixates on injustice, replaying the story over and over.
- The body carries tension, anger, frustration—long after the screen is turned off.

And yet, one returns again and again. The outrage cycle is addictive, not because it resolves anything, but because it provides the illusion of urgency.

To see this pattern clearly is to step outside of it. One begins to ask: Why am I feeding this? Why am I allowing my attention to be harvested for profit?

Self-Reflection: What would happen if I detoxed from outrage-driven media for just one week?

The Role of Confirmation Bias in Media Consumption

The unconscious mind does not seek truth—it seeks validation.

Each person believes that he is logical, objective, fair. And yet, the vast majority do not seek information—they seek confirmation. One does not search for news; one searches for agreement.

– The progressive finds the headlines that affirm his worldview.

– The conservative clicks on content that reinforces his beliefs.

– The reader scans for phrases that align with what he already thinks is true.

This is not conscious deception, but psychological conditioning. The mind clings to what feels familiar, what supports its preexisting narrative. And the media is well aware of this.

News outlets do not need to create entirely false stories—they only need to frame them in a way that their audience expects. A story can be real, and still be manipulated. The facts remain, but the perspective shifts.

– One detail is emphasized while another is omitted.

– A crime is reported differently depending on the identities of those involved.

– A protest is framed as "peaceful" or "violent," depending on who is reporting it.

The result? A population that believes itself to be informed, yet is merely affirmed in its own biases.

To awaken is to recognize this: To see how one seeks only what feels comfortable, never what challenges.

Self-Reflection: *Do I seek truth—or just validation? Am I brave enough to challenge my own biases—or do I just protect them?*

Breaking the Cycle of Engagement

If one wishes to break free from the media's manipulation, one must learn to starve the machine. The news cannot function without your participation. The outrage economy collapses when consumers choose to disengage.

This does not mean retreating into ignorance. It means becoming conscious of where one places attention.

> *"The most dangerous man to any government is the man who is able to think things out for himself, without regard to prevailing superstition or taboo."*
>
> *—H.L. Mencken*

Strategies for Resisting Outrage-Driven Media

Observe, but do not react.

Notice how media attempts to provoke you.

Recognize the emotional hooks in headlines and stories.

Ask: Why does this demand my reaction?

Consume with intention.

Do not allow news to be fed to you through algorithms.

Choose sources deliberately, rather than passively scrolling.

Seek multiple perspectives, not just the ones that feel comfortable.

Set boundaries.

Limit time spent on news and social media.

Notice when your body tenses in response to a story—step away.

Resist the urge to immediately share or react. Let the moment settle.

Question your own bias.

Ask: Do I believe this because it is true, or because it fits my worldview?

Be willing to sit with uncomfortable truths.

Recognize that certainty is often the enemy of understanding.

Outrage thrives on unconscious participation. The moment one becomes fully present, observing rather than reacting, the power of manipulation dissolves.

No longer controlled, no longer triggered, no longer feeding the system. In this state, one's attention becomes fully one's own.

Freedom does not come from avoiding information—it comes from seeing it clearly. And when you reclaim your attention, you reclaim your mind. That is the end of the outrage cycle. And that is true freedom.

Self-Reflection: If I only consumed media from the 'other side' for a week, how would my perspective shift?

The system thrives on reaction. The moment you observe rather than engage, its grip weakens.

The Societal Impact of Outrage-Driven Media

A person who is continuously exposed to outrage-driven media begins to perceive the world not as it is, but as it is framed—an endless conflict, a ceaseless battle of opposing forces. There is no room for stillness, no space for reflection, only reaction. This state of agitation creates division, erodes trust, and fuels an unconscious disengagement from reality itself.

The Polarization of Public Discourse

Outrage-driven media does not merely inform—it divides. The objective is not clarity but loyalty to a narrative. In this fragmented landscape, the goal is not to encourage understanding but to ensure that opposing perspectives appear irreconcilable.

When media rewards controversy, ideological camps harden. Individuals no longer interact as human beings, but as symbols of an ideology. Every discussion becomes a battlefield; every disagreement, an attack.

- Political debates turn into moral crusades where the other side is not simply wrong but evil.
- Minor policy differences escalate into cultural wars.
- Those who refuse to engage in the outrage are accused of complicity.

This is the architecture of division: a world in which outrage is currency and unity is weakness.

The consequences are profound. Nuance disappears. Debate collapses. Society fractures. A culture once capable of discourse dissolves into factions that see no value in conversation.

> *A society fueled by outrage loses the ability to think, speak, and listen with clarity.*

The Decline of Trust in Journalism

The moment an institution aligns itself with outrage, it ceases to function as a neutral observer. Journalism was once an attempt to uncover truth, but outrage does not seek truth—it seeks affirmation.

When outrage becomes profitable, the news ceases to be about information. It becomes a performance.

– Headlines are no longer written to inform, but to provoke.

– Reporters do not investigate; they interpret.

– Facts are not presented; they are curated.

Public trust in journalism has collapsed because journalism has collapsed into activism. A study on media trust found that faith in traditional news outlets has been steadily declining, particularly as viewers perceive growing partisanship in reporting.[14] The result is a population that no longer believes in the media's role as a neutral institution.

This does not mean that journalism is obsolete—far from it. Investigative reporting, independent media, and long-form journalism still serve as essential counterbalances. But they are drowned out by the noise of click-driven sensationalism. The challenge is not to reject all media, but to recognize when information is being presented to inform—and when it is being weaponized to provoke.

When trust erodes, people retreat into their own media bubbles, reinforcing their biases and ensuring that only familiar narratives are accepted.

"With the possible exception of things like box scores, race results, and stock market tabulations, there is no such thing as Objective Journalism."
—*Hunter S. Thompson*

The Rise of Cynicism and Disengagement

A society that is constantly provoked into emotional outrage eventually loses the ability to care. The nervous system cannot sustain a perpetual state of alarm. Exhaustion follows.

– People grow weary of every crisis being the "most urgent" crisis.

– Activism turns into fatigue.

– Voter turnout declines because people feel powerless.

The news cycle is relentless. Each day brings a new villain, a new scandal, a new existential threat. Yet, nothing seems to change. The outrage is immediate, but the resolution is nonexistent.

This creates a deep cynicism—a recognition that the media thrives on emotional manipulation, but an inability to escape it. Political apathy grows, not because issues are unimportant, but because constant exposure to outrage numbs the mind.

To step away from the cycle is to regain clarity.

To see the pattern is to break free from it.

> *When every moment is a crisis, no crisis is ever resolved.*

Self-Reflection: *What would change in my life if I spent less time reacting to manufactured outrage and more time cultivating inner stillness and clarity?*

Outrage Addiction Insight: Why You Can't Stop Clicking

Why is outrage-driven media so addictive? The answer lies in the brain's natural fear response—media outlets trigger the amygdala, creating a sense of urgency and danger that keeps people coming back for more.[15]

The brain's survival instincts are wired for alertness. When the media presents every news story as a threat, it keeps the nervous system in a state of activation. This is why people cannot resist doomscrolling, why they feel compelled to check the news, even when it causes distress.

> *The brain is wired for survival. Media exploits this by feeding it a constant loop of crisis and fear— because a fearful mind keeps clicking.*

Breaking free from this cycle does not mean withdrawing from the world—it means awakening to it. Awareness does not require avoidance; it requires clarity.

---

[15] *Tufekci, 2015; Zillmann, 2000*

When you step back, when you no longer feed the system with your attention, the illusion collapses. And in that collapse, you reclaim your mind.

REFLECTION: *Now ask yourself: How much of your anger is truly yours? And how much has been fed to you?*

Outrage Addiction Insight

Why are outrage-fueled headlines so hard to ignore?

Sensationalist media manipulates your amygdala, triggering fear and urgency responses.[16] This fear response increases cortisol levels and creates a heightened state of alertness. Each engagement—clicks, shares, or comments—rewards your brain with dopamine, reinforcing compulsive news consumption.[17]

---

[16] *Vuilleumier, 2005*
[17] *Zillmann, 2000*

Chapter Six

The Weaponization of Language

"Political language...is designed to make lies sound truthful and murder respectable."

— *George Orwell*

Language as the New Battleground

Language, at its most fundamental level, is a tool for communication—a bridge between minds. But when words cease to be vehicles of meaning and instead become instruments of power, language transforms from a tool of connection into a weapon of control.

Modern discourse is no longer about the free exchange of ideas but about who controls the terms. Meaning is no longer discovered—it is dictated. This is not the natural evolution of language but its deliberate manipulation.

> *Language shapes perception, but awareness remains free. Only the unconscious mind mistakes words for reality.*

How Words Have Evolved from Communication Tools to Instruments of Control

In its original purpose, language allowed societies to navigate truth collectively. Words named things as they were, providing clarity, precision, and a means of understanding. Today, words are increasingly used not to reveal reality but to reshape it according to ideological objectives.

- Dissenting opinions are no longer just "disagreements"—they are "violence."

- Challenging an accepted narrative is not "questioning"—it is "denialism."

- Language is policed, not for clarity, but for compliance.

This shift is not organic. It is an intentional strategy—one that reprograms the way people think, making them wary of questioning what they once understood instinctively. When language is controlled, perception follows.

Perception is not passive—it is shaped. The mind does not see reality as it is; it sees through the lens it has been given. Language shapes thought. But can thought exist beyond language?

Self-Reflection: Have you ever altered your words to avoid discomfort? What happens when silence becomes safer than truth?

The Redefinition of Language to Shape Reality

Language does not merely reflect reality—it shapes it. Those who dictate language hold power over how reality itself is framed. When terminology is altered to favor a particular ideology, it forces individuals to think within the parameters of that ideology, whether they agree with it or not.

- The shift from "sex" to "gender" redefined identity itself.

- The introduction of "micro-aggressions" transformed minor social slights into systemic oppression.

- The word "equity" replaced "equality" to change the very definition of fairness.

These shifts are not accidental. They function as linguistic Trojan horses, altering the way people engage with fundamental concepts. If a person accepts the term, they accept the ideological framework that accompanies it.

The Sapir-Whorf Hypothesis, a long-studied concept in linguistics, suggests that language determines the boundaries of thought.[1] When language is controlled, perception follows. If speech is controlled, so is the ability to question.

---

[1] *Whorf, 1956*

The Danger of Linguistic Manipulation in Fostering Ideological Conformity

There is a reason ideological movements seek to redefine language: control language, and you control the people. The power to dictate definitions determines what is considered acceptable thought.

- If questioning an idea is labeled "harm," people will censor themselves.

- If disagreeing is framed as "hate," debate becomes impossible.

- If words themselves are considered "dangerous," free speech no longer exists.

Modern discourse drifts from dialogue into linguistic compliance. The mind seeks safety in accepted words, mistaking conformity for truth.

Such conditions do not create a more just society. They create a culture of fear. People do not express what they truly believe—they say what they are permitted to say. This is not progress. It is regression into a world where language serves power rather than truth.

The reclaiming of honest discourse begins not with arguing about ideology but with refusing to surrender language itself.

Redefining Words: The Subtle Shift of Meaning

Language should reveal truth, not dictate it. The moment it does, it ceases to serve human understanding and becomes a tool of control.

The reshaping of words may appear subtle, but its effects are profound. By redefining language, perception itself is altered. Conversations shift, debate becomes constrained, and entire ideas become untouchable—not by reason but by linguistic decree. Language, once a means of exploration, becomes a means of enforcement.

The Power of Linguistic Framing

By carefully selecting which words to use and which meanings to ascribe to them, perception itself is steered. This is why political and ideological movements do not argue their positions as much as they reframe the language surrounding them.

- "Hate speech" once referred to explicit incitement of harm. Now, it is used to silence dissenting opinions.

- "Micro-aggression" reframes unintentional social missteps as acts of oppression.
- "Disinformation" is no longer a term for factual inaccuracies but for ideas that challenge approved narratives.

These changes are not neutral. They guide thought in predetermined directions. To question them is to question the very frame of reality they impose. This is why ideological movements place such emphasis on language—not as a means of communication but as a means of behavioral conditioning.

By altering the meaning of a word, an entire conversation is redefined.

> *Words do not shape reality, only our perception of it. Reality remains untouched by language.*

Reality remains unchanged, yet perception bends to language. The conditioned mind sees only through the lens it has been given. Yet awareness exists beyond words—untouched, unshaped, beyond interpretation.

Self-Reflection: *Have you noticed how the meaning of words shifts? What happens when language dictates what may be seen?*

Inflation of Terms: From Disagreement to 'Violence'

Once, violence was an act of physical aggression—something measurable and undeniable. Today, violence is redefined to include words, ideas, and even silence. This is not a linguistic evolution—it is a linguistic inflation.

– Disagreement is framed as "harm."

– Challenging an idea is labeled as "oppression."

– Failing to affirm a position is cast as an "act of violence."

This inflation does not expand understanding—it destroys distinctions. If words are violence, then speech is a weapon. If offense is harm, then ideas must be policed. If questioning is oppression, then debate itself becomes a crime.

> *When words are mistaken for harm, silence becomes survival.*

The problem with this inflation is that it erodes the seriousness of real harm. If being disagreed with is the same as being attacked, then actual victims of violence and oppression are no longer distinguishable from those experiencing momentary discomfort.

This is not progress. It is the dilution of meaning itself.

The mind, conditioned by language, sees only through its given lens. Yet awareness remains beyond words—unshaped, unbound.

Self-Reflection: Do you speak from truth or from fear of consequence?

The Psychological Impact of Language Manipulation

Language, when altered, does not merely change conversations—it changes minds, not by persuasion, but by coercion. When words are redefined, the boundaries of acceptable thought are redrawn.

– If a term is made emotionally charged, it evokes fear—making dissent emotionally costly.

– If a concept is rebranded as harmful, people self-censor—not because they agree, but because they are afraid.

– If a word carries social consequences, then refusing to use it invites social exile.

This is how language dictates compliance. The emotional weight of a word is manipulated to elicit automatic reactions.

– "If I say this, will I be punished?"

– "If I question this, will I be cast out?"

– "If I remain silent, will I still be guilty?"

This is not free thought. It is a behavioral conditioning system. By controlling the definitions of words, individuals do not need to be forced into submission. They will submit voluntarily, fearing the consequences of deviation.

> *When thought believes in the power of words, it begins to police itself.*

When language is constrained, thought contracts. A mind afraid to question becomes rigid, repeating what it knows. But awareness is not thought. Beneath language, stillness remains.

This is the deeper cost of manipulated language. It does not only alter conversations. It alters the individual.

Cancel Culture: The Social Punishment for Perceived Offenses

Cancel culture is often framed as a form of social justice—a way of holding individuals accountable for their words and actions. But beneath this justification lies something deeper: a psychological and cultural mechanism that punishes perceived ideological deviation. What begins as a call for responsibility often escalates into public shaming, professional exile, and social isolation.

Accountability considers intent and context. Cancel culture does not. It delivers judgment instantly—without deliberation, without redemption.

Defining Cancel Culture

Societies have always ostracized dissenters. What makes modern cancel culture distinct is its scale, speed, and permanence.

Social media once amplified marginalized voices and held institutions accountable. But what began as a tool for justice has become an instrument of ideological control.

- The goal of cancel culture is no longer simply to correct behavior—it is to eliminate dissent.

- The power of cancel culture lies in its immediacy—judgment is rendered swiftly, without context or due process.

- The consequences are often disproportionate—an individual's entire reputation, career, or social standing can be erased in a moment.

Cancel culture does not just punish—it warns. To witness someone being canceled is to internalize a lesson—stay silent, conform, or risk the same fate.

> *The mind, fearing rejection, trades truth for belonging.*

The distinction between accountability and cancellation is crucial. Genuine accountability allows for growth, learning, and redemption. Cancel culture demands absolute purity, and even a misstep from decades past can justify total social expulsion.

Conversation opens space. Crusades close it. Where there is listening, dialogue unfolds. Where certainty prevails, enforcement follows. The mind insists that certainty is strength, but true strength is found in stillness, not in force.

The Dynamics of Public Shaming

What makes cancel culture so effective—so deeply feared—is the way digital platforms amplify and sustain public shaming. In earlier societies, ostracization was localized; it was contained within a community and often reversible. Today, the internet ensures that cancellation is permanent.

How Digital Platforms Enable Shaming and Ostracism

Social Media as a Courtroom

Platforms like Twitter and Facebook allow for mass condemnation in real-time.

The accused is often stripped of any ability to respond before judgment is finalized.

The Role of Anonymity

Many of those who participate in cancel culture do so under pseudonyms.

The ability to shame without consequence emboldens even those who might hesitate in real-world interactions.

The Speed of Viral Punishment

A minor comment, a past tweet, or even a private message can be resurfaced and turned into national outrage.

Within hours, calls for firing, deplatforming, and boycotting can escalate into corporate and institutional action.

The Disproportionate Consequences of Cancellation

Unlike traditional social consequences, which often include paths to reconciliation, cancellation operates on a zero-tolerance basis. The cost is rarely equivalent to the offense.

> – A comedian loses their career over a decade-old joke.

> – A professor is fired for discussing an academic topic that becomes politically inconvenient.

> – A private citizen is doxxed, harassed, and threatened for a comment taken out of context.

Each example reveals the same pattern: punishment is not about dialogue, correction, or improvement. It is about public submission.

An accusation becomes guilt. Doubt is condemned, not explored. The mind, conditioned by fear, does not pause to question—only to condemn. But truth does not arise through force. It emerges in the stillness beyond reaction, where the need to be right dissolves, and clarity remains.

The result? Silence. People grow more cautious about what they say, not out of genuine respect or understanding but out of fear of exile.

Self-Reflection: *When you speak, does it arise from presence or from conditioned thought?*

Notable Examples of Cancel Culture in Action

The names change, but the script remains the same. Across media, academia, and corporate spaces, cancel culture has claimed individuals for perceived ideological infractions—often without recourse.

Case Study 1: J.K. Rowling and the Boundaries of Acceptable Speech

In 2020, acclaimed author J.K. Rowling came under fire for comments regarding gender and biological sex. What began as a debate over women's identity and language escalated into calls for her books to be banned, for publishers to cut ties, and for charities to refuse her donations.

> - Despite her longstanding progressive advocacy, a single issue became the defining measure of her moral standing.

> - Fellow authors and industry figures distanced themselves out of fear of association.

- Her cancellation became a test of ideological loyalty—silence meant complicity, defense meant self-sacrifice.

Her case exemplifies how cancel culture does not weigh past contributions—one misalignment with prevailing orthodoxy can render an individual irredeemable.

Case Study 2: Nicholas Christakis and the Yale Halloween Controversy

In 2015, Yale professor Nicholas Christakis and his wife Erika faced backlash for an email suggesting that students should handle potentially offensive Halloween costumes with personal discussion rather than institutional regulation.

– The response was swift and furious—protests erupted, students demanded resignations and social media campaigns labeled them complicit in harmful discourse.

- Despite being highly regarded academics, the couple was pressured to step down from leadership positions.

- The message was clear: even the mildest questioning of ideological norms was punishable.

Christakis later reflected that the incident was not about costumes but about control—the ability to dictate the limits of acceptable conversation.[2]

Case Study 3: David Shor and the Demand for Political Purity

In 2020, data analyst David Shor was fired from his job at a progressive firm after tweeting a study by a Black Princeton professor showing that violent protests tend to decrease public support for political movements.

- The study was academically valid but uncomfortable to activists who believed all protest methods should be unquestioned.

- His crime was not falsehood but inconvenient truth.

- Despite working for progressive causes, one tweet led to his cancellation.

His case reveals a key paradox of cancel culture: even those who align politically with the movement can be discarded if they express a thought that disrupts the approved narrative.

The Long-Term Consequences of Cancellation

The effects of cancel culture go beyond the individual. They reshape entire

---

institutions, stifling discourse and creating environments governed by fear rather than reason.

Self-Censorship Becomes the Norm

Individuals avoid discussing certain topics, not because they have changed their views, but because the risk of cancellation is too great.

Intellectual Rigor Declines

Universities, media outlets, and workplaces prioritize ideological compliance over inquiry—stifling creativity and growth.

A Culture of Fear Replaces Open Discourse

Public spaces become less about truth-seeking and more about avoiding social condemnation.

Truth does not defend itself. The mind fears consequences, mistaking disapproval for annihilation. Yet truth remains, untouched by consensus.

Cancel culture is not about justice. It is about power. It is not about dialogue. It is about enforcement. And in its wake, a quieter, more fearful, and less intellectually honest society remains.

"The limits of my language mean the limits of my world."
— Ludwig Wittgenstein

The Language of Control: Enforcing Conformity Through Speech

Language is not merely a tool of communication; it is a mechanism of influence. Words shape perception, dictate narratives, and, when controlled, enforce ideological conformity. In societies where free thought is discouraged, language becomes the battleground. By redefining terms, silencing deviation, and embedding ideological litmus tests into everyday speech, control is exerted without the need for direct coercion.

In this environment, disagreement is not met with discussion but with enforced silence. The mere act of questioning certain terms can lead to ostracization. Words once meant to describe reality are repurposed to dictate it.

> *Thought, believing itself to be language, bends to its definitions.*

Ideological Litmus Tests in Language

Once a scientific concept, the litmus test is now a social requirement. Speech is no longer about communication—it is a marker of ideological alignment.

Certain phrases act as passwords into respectable discourse, while others signal deviance. Words and their evolving definitions dictate who belongs and who does not. This is most evident in academic, corporate, and political environments, where the use of the "correct" terminology is often a condition for participation.

Academia: Universities have increasingly introduced speech codes that dictate the acceptable framing of ideas. Professors and students alike navigate conversations carefully, knowing that using an outdated or politically incorrect term—no matter how innocently—can result in disciplinary action.

Corporate Culture: In major companies, Diversity, Equity, and Inclusion (DEI) training often includes specific linguistic expectations. Words like "meritocracy" are quietly discouraged, while terms like "lived experience" carry authoritative weight, requiring no empirical substantiation.

Political Spaces: Public figures are expected to adhere to prevailing linguistic trends or risk backlash. A politician who fails to use the latest iteration of an identity-related term may be labeled regressive or even bigoted.

Language, once a means of discovery, is now a means of control. Those who refuse to conform face social and professional exile.

Self-Reflection: When have you traded authenticity for approval?

Censorship by Rebranding Language

Control over language does not always manifest in explicit censorship. More often, it emerges through rebranding—a quiet but deliberate process of shifting meanings to obscure uncomfortable realities.

A word once meant to describe a concrete reality is given a new, more palatable interpretation. Consider the following examples:

"Equity" vs. "Equality"
– Equality traditionally referred to fairness—the idea that individuals should have equal opportunities.

– Equity, now commonly used in policy language, suggests engineered outcomes—redistributing resources to ensure proportional results.

– The shift is subtle but profound: where once the focus was on equal rights, the emphasis now is on predetermined results.

"Violence" and "Harm"
– Physical violence and psychological harm were once clearly defined. Today, speech itself is often labeled as violence, collapsing the distinction between words and actions.

– This redefinition allows for suppression: if disagreement can be framed as "harm," then silencing dissent is framed as "protection."

"Justice" and "Social Justice"
– Justice was long understood as an impartial process based on individual accountability.

– Social justice reframes it as collective responsibility, where guilt or innocence is assigned based on group identity rather than individual action.

This linguistic shift is not accidental. It ensures that those who question the new definitions are accused of opposing the underlying values. To challenge the new meaning of "equity" is to be against fairness. To resist the inflation of "violence" is to be indifferent to suffering. The terms, now imbued with ideological weight, serve as a tool for silencing debate.

The Cost of Linguistic Conformity

The pressure to conform linguistically has consequences far beyond the words themselves. It affects free thought, creativity, and intellectual exploration. When words are policed, ideas are stifled.

The Decline of Open Discourse: The range of acceptable speech narrows, discouraging people from asking genuine questions. In classrooms, workplaces, and public forums, self-censorship becomes instinctive.

Creativity is Crushed: Writers, artists, and comedians must navigate their craft within shrinking linguistic boundaries. A misplaced word can mean professional destruction.

Psychological Toll: The fear of saying the wrong thing creates an environment of constant vigilance, leading to stress and anxiety. People hesitate to speak, fearing that one misstep might lead to career or social ruin.

Censorship is most effective when it is internalized. When individuals police their own thoughts, the enforcers of conformity are no longer needed. The system sustains itself.

The mind shapes language, and language shapes the mind. Thought may contract, but awareness remains spacious. No word can limit what is beyond words. It remains silent and vast, beyond what language seeks to contain

In this landscape, the choice is clear: either conform to the prescribed language or risk being cast out.

Reclaiming the Power of Language for Open Discourse

Language does not just express thought—it shapes perception. When language is dictated rather than discovered, thought is no longer an organic process—it is shaped before it can even begin. To reclaim intellectual freedom, we must first reclaim our relationship with language.

The Importance of Precision and Clarity in Public Dialogue

When words lose their meaning, communication becomes impossible. In a culture where definitions shift according to ideological trends, conversations cease to be about mutual understanding and become battles over who controls the narrative.

Precision in language is not an abstract concern—it determines how ideas are received, how policies are shaped, and how societies function. Consider the difference between the words "equality" and "equity" or "justice" and "social justice." These terms, though seemingly related, have been repurposed to serve ideological ends, leaving the average person confused about what is actually being proposed.

A call for "safety" may be used to suppress speech. A plea for "justice" may demand collective guilt rather than individual responsibility. Without precision, language becomes a tool of manipulation rather than a means of communication.

To reclaim open discourse, we must first insist on clarity. Words must mean what they mean, not what ideological forces wish them to mean.

> *Truth does not require clarity, only the absence of distortion.*

Resisting Ideological Manipulation Through Conscious Language Use

The first step in resisting manipulation is recognizing it. This requires conscious attention to the language used in media, institutions, and public debate.

Ask:

- Has the definition of this word changed recently?
- Does this term clarify meaning, or does it obscure it?
- Would this idea hold the same weight if it were expressed in plain, neutral language?

For example, when a person is accused of committing "verbal violence," ask whether the language itself has been manipulated to equate words with physical harm. If "misinformation" is used to silence dissent rather than to correct falsehoods, question whether the goal is truth—or control.

By questioning imposed language, we reclaim independent thought.

***Self-Reflection:** What words have you absorbed without question? What happens when you pause before believing them?*

Fostering Intellectual Freedom Through Linguistic Honesty

True intellectual freedom cannot exist in an environment where speech is dictated by ideological conformity. The moment language is restricted, thought is constrained. Yet, the solution is not to engage in the same ideological games but to return to something far simpler: honesty in language.

This means:

- Speaking plainly rather than performatively. Avoiding jargon that obscures rather than clarifies.

- Refusing to self-censor out of fear. Expressing ideas clearly, even when they challenge dominant narratives.

- Defending the right to discuss difficult topics. Not allowing debates to be shut down by linguistic intimidation.

Courage in speech is not about being inflammatory—it is about refusing to surrender truth to coercion. The goal is not to weaponize words in return but to restore language to its rightful role: a vehicle for thought, not a tool of ideological enforcement.

Linguistic control holds power only when accepted. Step beyond words, and it dissolves.

"Language is the apparel in which your thoughts parade before the public."   — *George W. Crane*

Outrage Addiction Insight

Why does emotionally charged language feel so powerful?

The strategic use of loaded language activates emotional responses by stimulating the amygdala and triggering stress reactions.[3] When words like "violence" or "oppression" are redefined and used in provocative contexts, they intensify emotional engagement. Each emotional reaction strengthens the dopamine reward loop, creating an addictive attachment to outrage-driven narratives.[4]

---

[3] *Lakoff, 2004*
[4] *Citron & Norton, 2011*

We'd Love to Hear From You!

Thank you so much for reading this book-it means the world to me. If you found it helpful, inspiring, or just enjoyable, would you take a moment to leave a review? Your feedback not only helps others but also keeps me motivated to create more valuable content for you.

Here's how you can leave a review:

1. Scan the QR code on this page to go directly to the author's page.

2. Or, visit your Amazon Orders page, find this book, and click "Write a Product Review."

**Your kind words make a big difference.
Thank you for your support!**

Consequences of Outrage Addiction

"Anger is an acid that can do more harm to the vessel in which it is stored than to anything on which it is poured."

— Mark Twain

The Emotional Toll of Constant Outrage

Why does outrage linger long after the moment has passed? Why does it echo in the body, disrupt sleep, tighten the chest? This chapter isn't about what we see in the world—it's about what we carry. The cost of outrage is not only social. It is deeply personal.

Outrage, when habitual, ceases to be a response and becomes a state of being. It is no longer the fleeting reaction to an injustice but the baseline emotional state, an identity formed around grievance. This is not an accident, nor is it without consequence.

> *Living in a constant state of offense doesn't signal awareness—it signals exhaustion dressed up as virtue.*

The modern individual, constantly engaged with cycles of digital outrage, finds themselves in a state of perpetual emotional arousal—fueling a psychological addiction that mimics the characteristics of substance dependency.[1]

---

[1] *Potenza et al., 2019*

Outrage as a Psychological and Emotional Addiction

The mind, when exposed to repetitive patterns of stimulation, adapts accordingly. Outrage triggers the brain's reward system. A fleeting rush of satisfaction, the illusion of power. Social media amplifies this, feeding what provokes the strongest reaction.

> *Outrage feels powerful in the moment, but over time it erodes the very energy needed for real change.*

The more one engages, the more the mind craves. And soon, anger is no longer a response to injustice, but a need—an unconscious pull toward the next emotional high.

Why Outrage Feels "Right" (Even When It's Not)

Outrage is not just an emotional reaction. It is a shortcut. The mind, overwhelmed by complexity, craves certainty. And in that craving, it latches onto outrage, mistaking it for truth. But certainty is an illusion—one sustained by a series of unconscious distortions.

The mind resists nuance. It prefers clear divisions—good and evil, right and wrong, us and them. It convinces itself that disagreement is not just wrong but irredeemable. That those who think differently must be opposed, not understood. But is this truth, or is it simply the mind's need for control? Certainty is rigid. It contracts, resists, rejects. The moment the mind believes it already knows, it stops listening. The instant contraction, the shutting down of possibility? And in that noticing—can you step back? Can you allow for something beyond certainty?

Outrage is not random. It is chosen. The mind, conditioned by habit, seeks what affirms its beliefs while discarding what challenges them. The result? Certainty mistaken for truth, conflict mistaken for clarity.[2] And so, selective exposure becomes mistaken for truth. The world shrinks. The mind hardens. And yet, the craving remains.

Outrage mimics moral certainty. The angrier one is, the more righteous they feel. But is this virtue—or just another form of intoxication?

And then, there is the validation. Outrage is not only internal; it is rewarded. The more aggressively someone expresses their indignation, the more likes, shares,

---

[2] *Nickerson, 1998*

and approval they receive. And with each echo of agreement, a false sense of consensus grows. Everyone agrees with me. Anyone who doesn't is ignorant or evil. But is this real agreement? Or is it simply the mind being fed what it already believes?

These distortions do not lead to truth. They trap the mind in a righteous loop, where questioning outrage feels like betrayal. And yet, the moment one steps back—even for an instant—the illusion weakens. There is space. And in that space, clarity.

Righteousness feels good. It hardens certainty, silences doubt. But does it reveal truth—or obscure it?

The Illusion of Empowerment Through Outrage

There is a profound irony in the addictive nature of outrage. It masquerades as empowerment—offering a sense of control, moral clarity, and purpose—yet it ultimately diminishes personal agency.

> *The reactive mind is never free; it is shackled to the next perceived offense, the next controversy, the next demand for moral positioning.*

The reactive mind is never free; it is shackled to the next perceived offense, the next controversy, the next demand for moral positioning. A life of outrage is a life of reaction. One's emotions no longer belong to them but are dictated by headlines, arguments, and the need to be seen on the 'right' side. This is not autonomy. It is dcpcndcncc.

The Hidden Personal Cost

Outrage lingers. Even after the argument is over, the mind remains restless, primed for the next fight. Small disagreements become battles. Every conversation carries the weight of past grievances.

When outrage becomes habitual, a quiet exhaustion sets in. The joy once found in simple moments fades. Conversations lose warmth. The mind, once open to curiosity, becomes rigid. Outrage continues—not because it brings clarity, but because the mind no longer knows how to be without it. Can you feel this in yourself? Can you recognize the cost?

The cost is not only internal. Relationships deteriorate under the weight of perpetual indignation. Conversations become battlegrounds, loved ones become ideological adversaries, and the ability to engage with nuance erodes. Those who build their identity around outrage find themselves increasingly isolated—not because the world has become more unjust, but because their threshold for tolerance has been lowered to an unsustainable degree.

Freedom from outrage is not apathy. It is action without reactivity. Clarity without compulsion.

Without this realization, outrage remains a hollow substitute for real agency, keeping individuals locked in a cycle of emotional dependency, forever mistaking their own reactivity for righteousness.

The Mental Health Toll: Anxiety, Depression, and Emotional Fatigue

The human mind is not designed to live in a perpetual state of agitation, yet modern outrage culture demands precisely that. The continuous engagement with inflammatory content—be it through media, social platforms, or public discourse—keeps individuals in a state of psychological arousal that is neither natural nor sustainable.

What begins as an emotional reaction to perceived injustice soon becomes an enduring mental burden, manifesting in anxiety, exhaustion, and a gradual erosion of well-being.

The Emotional Cost of Living on High Alert

Chronic engagement with outrage keeps the nervous system in a prolonged fight-or-flight state. Have you noticed the tension in your body when outrage arises? The tightness in the chest, the quickening of breath, the sense of urgency? The body does not distinguish between an immediate physical threat and a thought it finds unacceptable. The reaction is the same. But you can step back and see this. You can notice that the suffering is not in the event but in the reaction to it. And the moment you see this, a space opens. And in that space, peace.

The mind does not distinguish between an immediate danger and an idea it finds unacceptable. Both are treated as threats. The body reacts—tension, rapid breath, the pulse quickening. Yet there is no danger, only thought. A comment, an opinion, a fleeting moment on a screen. But the mind holds onto it, replaying the grievance, feeding the outrage. Can you observe this? Can you see that the suffering is not in the event but in the reaction to it? The moment this is seen, the pattern weakens. In that awareness, there is space. And in that space, peace.

The Suppression of Intellectual Freedom: Emotional Reactivity and Thought Narrowing

As the individual becomes more entrenched in emotional reactivity, the mind begins to suppress its own capacity for critical thinking and intellectual exploration. Just as outrage narrows emotional experiences, it simultaneously narrows mental ones. Reactions become automatic, and the willingness to question, explore, or even listen fades. What was once a dynamic, open mind becomes rigid, controlled by external triggers and internal patterns of thought that no longer allow for dissent or inquiry.

> *Outrage, when habitual, ceases to be a response and becomes a state of being, an identity formed around grievance, diminishing the capacity for open, critical thought*

This narrowing of thought creates a parallel to the societal pressures we face to conform to ideological purity. When outrage becomes habitual, individuals are conditioned to accept predefined positions without question, often rejecting alternative viewpoints. This process—where questioning and intellectual exploration are suppressed in favor of conformity—mirrors the cultural forces that increasingly discourage free thought and dissent in the wider world.

Outrage Fatigue and Compassion Burnout

There is a profound contradiction in outrage culture: the demand for moral engagement is constant, yet the capacity for sustained emotional investment is limited. The result is compassion fatigue, a phenomenon in which individuals, overwhelmed by the sheer volume of injustice and suffering they are expected to process, begin to emotionally shut down.[3]

---

[3] *(Figley, 2002).*

> *Outrage feels powerful in the moment, but over time, it weakens the mental and emotional energy needed for true engagement and meaningful change.*

Healthcare professionals, social workers, and activists have long been familiar with this form of exhaustion. But in the age of digital activism, where participation is demanded not just from those directly involved in a cause but from all individuals at all times, compassion fatigue has become widespread. The expectation to react—to display concern, to express indignation—places a relentless burden on the psyche. Eventually, the mind, overwhelmed by its inability to fix everything it perceives as wrong, detaches as a means of self-preservation.

This detachment, however, does not bring peace. Instead, it manifests as cynicism, apathy, and an increasing sense of despair. When everything is framed as an emergency, nothing truly feels solvable, and the result is emotional paralysis.

Psychological Insights: Cognitive Dissonance and Anxiety

The cycle of outrage addiction mirrors the psychological effects of suppression and fear. When we engage constantly with outrage, we begin to experience cognitive dissonance—our actions are out of alignment with our deeper need for intellectual freedom. The stress and anxiety that accompany this dissonance fuel a mind-state where reaction becomes habitual, and questioning ceases. As individuals, we feel the pressure to maintain outrage, believing it is a form of moral engagement, but deep down, it only intensifies our emotional and intellectual exhaustion.

Compassion fatigue also aligns with this phenomenon. The mind becomes overwhelmed not only by the external demand for constant reaction but also by the internal conflict it generates. As individuals, we are trapped in a cycle of emotional consumption, where we react without truly engaging with the complexities of the issues. This emotional overload, compounded by the inability to fix every perceived injustice, creates a sense of anxiety and stress that feeds into the detachment we experience as a defense mechanism.

The Rise of Digital Burnout

The human mind is not meant to process an infinite stream of conflict, yet digital consumption ensures that it does. Unlike previous generations, where outrage was often confined to specific moments—a news broadcast, a conversation, an article—the modern individual is confronted with it every time they check their phone. This leads to a unique form of digital burnout, where the constant influx of polarizing content diminishes cognitive function and emotional regulation.[4]

Outrage is not free. It costs focus, rest, and well-being. The more one consumes it, the more depleted they become. The very platforms that promise connection and awareness become sources of psychological strain.

Breaking free from this cycle does not mean disengagement from the world—it means disengagement from the compulsive need to react. The media profits from outrage, but engagement is still a choice. The constant pull to react is not external—it is internal, conditioned by repeated exposure. Studies show that individuals who consciously limit their interaction with outrage-driven content experience lower stress levels and greater emotional stability.[5] The question is not whether outrage exists in the media—it always will—but whether one chooses to be consumed by it. The power of disengagement is not in avoidance but in reclaiming attention from those who seek to manipulate it for profit.

The mind, left unchecked, will chase validation through outrage, seeking the high of righteous anger and the social reward of agreement. True awareness, however, does not require exhaustion. The ability to perceive injustice without being consumed by it is a form of inner liberation, one that allows for clarity, action, and peace. Without this, outrage remains an endless cycle—one that ultimately depletes the very individuals it claims to empower.

Stepping away from outrage addiction does not mean ignoring the world's problems or suppressing righteous anger. It means choosing when to engage and when to detach. It means recognizing that constant emotional reactivity is neither productive nor necessary.

Relationship Breakdown: How Outrage Erodes Personal Connections

A mind trapped in outrage does not listen. It waits to react. Outrage thrives on separation, not unity. It convinces people that ideological purity is more important than love, that moral superiority is more important than understanding. The result is fractured families, friendships turned into battlegrounds, and communities divided by rigid ideological walls.

---

[4] Tufekci, 2017
[5] Orben et al., 2019

Outrage in Close Relationships

Have you noticed how outrage separates? How, in its presence, connection dissolves? A conversation becomes a battleground. A friend becomes an opponent. A loved one becomes a symbol of everything you stand against. The mind believes it is protecting something—an idea, a truth, a cause. But what is lost in the process? Can you see how outrage does not unite, but isolates? Can you step back, even for a moment, and see the other person—not as an argument to be won, but as they are?

> *Outrage isolates, turning human connection into ideological combat—what once united people is now a battleground driven by moral superiority, rather than understanding.*

The role of moral superiority in this breakdown cannot be overstated. When one person sees themselves as the enlightened one, and the other as an ignorant or morally deficient adversary, there is no room for mutual respect. Disagreement is no longer discussion. It is war. A difference of opinion is seen as betrayal, and ideological purity is valued over connection. A relative, a colleague, a friend—someone you once laughed with—now feels like an adversary. And why? Because they think differently? When did conversation become combat? When did understanding become betrayal? The mind, caught in outrage, sees only separation. It divides—right and wrong, good and bad, us and them. But who suffers most from this division? And what happens if you refuse to participate in it?[6] When ideological identity overrides human connection, love is replaced by contempt, and dialogue is replaced by denunciation.

The Erosion of Empathy in Personal Interactions

Empathy requires stillness. It requires presence. But the mind addicted to outrage does not allow for such stillness; it is always looking for the next offense, the next proof that it is on the right side of history. In this state, empathy is cast aside in favor of performance—proving to others that one is morally correct becomes more important than actually understanding another's experience.

Outrage does not connect—it separates. It turns friends into enemies, family members into adversaries. It convinces you that understanding is weakness, that

---

[6] *Finkel et al., 2020*

forgiveness is betrayal. But what happens when you let go of this belief? When you meet another human being not as an opponent, but as they are? In that moment, division disappears—not because the other person has changed, but because you no longer need them to."

This rejection is not rooted in thoughtful disagreement but in an unwillingness to risk ideological contamination. The culture of public condemnation further discourages empathy—expressing any form of understanding for the "wrong" group is seen as betrayal.

In this way, outrage culture suppresses not just open discussion but the ability to see one another as human beings beyond political labels. Forgiveness, once considered a virtue, is now framed as complicity. Compassion is seen as weakness. The result is a society where people fear genuine connection because it might force them to confront the humanity of those they have been told to despise.

But division is only a construct of the mind. It is not real. Beyond thought, beyond identity, beyond the conditioned belief that "they" are different from "me," connection already exists. It is not something that must be built—it only needs to be uncovered.

Daryl Davis, a black musician, did not seek to defeat his adversaries. He did not meet hatred with counter-hatred. He simply sat with those who had been conditioned to despise him, listening without the need to correct, to argue, to impose. And in that space of stillness, transformation occurred—not through force, but through presence. Over 200 members of the *Ku Klux Klan* left their robes behind, not because they were persuaded, but because they saw—perhaps for the first time—the illusion they had been living in.[7]

Or take the relationship between Ruth Bader Ginsburg and Antonin Scalia. The mind would say they were opposites, their views irreconcilable. Yet in their presence together, beyond ideology, beyond the constant push to be right, there was laughter, warmth, shared experience. Their friendship was not in spite of their differences but beyond them—untouched by the need to prove, to persuade, to win.[8]

The mind believes relationships must be fixed. But they were never broken— only obscured by perception. Reconnection is not about proving a point; it is about seeing past division.

---

[7] *Davis D, 1998*
[8] *Ginsburg, R. B.,2016*

Real-Life Examples of Relationships Fractured by Outrage

There is no shortage of stories where ideological rigidity has torn relationships apart. Consider the case of Jodi Shaw, a former employee at Smith College, who publicly resigned after she was pressured to affirm ideological beliefs that conflicted with her personal convictions. Her stance led to social ostracization, not only from her workplace but from personal circles as well.[9]

Or take the case of author J.K. Rowling, whose comments on gender and feminism led to public denouncements, including by actors who owed their careers to her work. Fans who once cherished her books as part of their childhoods severed their emotional connection to her work entirely. It was not enough to disagree with her; she had to be erased.

Even in private settings, this pattern emerges. A survey conducted by the American Enterprise Institute found that nearly one-third of Americans have either lost friendships or experienced strain in relationships due to political differences.[10] These are not theoretical debates; they are lived experiences—siblings who no longer speak, lifelong friends who have blocked one another, marriages that crumble under the pressure of ideological purity tests.

The Path to Reconnection

If outrage is allowed to dominate human relationships, the result is a lonely world where people become increasingly divided and isolated.

Awareness and Reconnection: Seeing Beyond the Ego's Need to Divide

The mind, conditioned by outrage, believes it must fix relationships in order to restore connection. But in truth, connection is never lost—it is only obscured by mental noise, by the incessant identification with thought, with belief, with ideology. The mind says, "They are wrong. I am right." And so, division persists.

But the deeper reality is that relationships are not broken—only perception is. When you drop the mental narratives about who someone is, about what they represent, about how they should think, a space opens. In that space, connection already exists. It does not need to be rebuilt; it only needs to be recognized.

Observe How the Mind Seeks Conflict.

Notice the moment when anger arises in a conversation with another. The need

---

[9] *Shaw, 2021*
[10] *Doherty & Kiley, 2020*

to defend. The impulse to correct. The silent judgment: "How could they think this way?" Do not suppress it—simply watch. Is this truly you speaking? Or is it the conditioned mind, the accumulation of past grievances and opinions that you have mistaken for yourself?

If you were to let go of the thought, "This person must understand me," what remains?

Only presence.

Only stillness.

Only the direct experience of another human being, free from the weight of past arguments.

This is the path of reconnection. Not persuasion. Not proving a point. Just presence. The present moment does not recognize division—it only sees what is. And in that seeing, separation dissolves.

ooooo

The ego thrives on conflict, on maintaining the illusion that some relationships are irreparably broken. But if you let go of the story—if you stop feeding the mind's need for opposition—you may discover that the person you thought you had lost was never gone. They were only hidden beneath layers of thought.

When the impulse to react arises, see it for what it is—just a thought, just a movement of the conditioned mind. If you do not engage with it, it fades. And in its absence, you may notice something unexpected—peace, stillness, the quiet presence of another human being. What happens to division when the mind no longer clings to it?

The Illusion of Control: Why Outrage Doesn't Empower You

A mind consumed by outrage believes it is powerful. It feels righteous, in control, and certain that it is shaping the world. Yet, this belief is an illusion. The pursuit of justice through anger often disguises a deeper reality—powerlessness. Outrage becomes an emotional crutch, a way to impose a sense of control over an unpredictable world. But instead of true influence, it leads only to exhaustion, bitterness, and a dependency on conflict.

The False Sense of Agency

The mind caught in outrage believes it is doing something. By denouncing, condemning, or demanding change, it feels engaged in the world. But is this real power, or is it merely a performance—an illusion that mimics action without producing meaningful results? Consider the waves of online outrage that spark viral movements, demand apologies, and call for boycotts. Does this truly change the structures of power, or does it merely provide a fleeting sense of participation?

The truth is that much of modern outrage does not create lasting change; it creates engagement. Social media platforms reward outrage, amplifying voices that express anger because they generate more clicks, shares, and comments. This makes the user feel involved, but in reality, the engagement benefits corporations, not individuals.

> *The illusion of control through outrage misleads the mind into believing it is engaged, while in reality, it only contributes to exhaustion and emotional burnout.*

This illusion of control is deeply psychological. When people feel powerless in their own lives, they often seek external conflicts where they can assert dominance. Outrage becomes a substitute for direct engagement with real challenges. Instead of building, they destroy. Instead of deepening understanding, they demand submission. Yet, when the anger subsides, the world remains unchanged—except for the emotional exhaustion left behind.

The Trap of Perpetual Victimhood

A person who sees themselves as a victim of constant injustice will remain in a state of suffering, regardless of external changes. Outrage culture reinforces this mindset by framing every disagreement as oppression, every inconvenience as violence. When individuals view themselves as perpetual victims, they surrender their own agency, believing that their happiness, peace, and security are always in the hands of others.

This belief is not only limiting but deeply destructive. It prevents personal growth, replaces resilience with fragility, and conditions people to seek grievance instead of solutions. Have you noticed the weight of helplessness? The voice in the mind that says, "There's nothing I can do"? The shrinking, the giving up, the waiting for someone else to fix things? The more this belief is fed, the stronger it becomes. And so, action is replaced by complaint. Clarity is replaced by resentment. The world seems unjust, oppressive—yet beneath the outrage, there is something deeper. A quiet resignation. A sense that nothing will ever change. But is this true? Or is it simply the mind, conditioned by repetition, mistaking powerlessness for reality? They become dependent on outrage, not to enact real change, but to validate their sense of victimhood.

A striking example of this phenomenon can be seen in the outrage cycles surrounding public apologies. An individual or company makes a controversial statement, the internet erupts in outrage, a demand for an apology ensues, and the apology is issued. But does this resolve the problem? Rarely. Instead, it fuels another wave of outrage—either because the apology is deemed insufficient or because it is framed as insincere. This cycle continues indefinitely, reinforcing a pattern where those outraged remain in a state of perpetual grievance, unable to move forward.

Emotional Dependency on Outrage Cycles

The cycle of outrage operates like any other addiction. It begins with a trigger—an article, a tweet, a news story—that elicits an emotional reaction. That reaction is validated by likes, comments, and shares, creating a temporary high. But as with any high, it fades. To recapture that sense of righteousness and purpose, the individual seeks another trigger. Over time, they become dependent on outrage, mistaking it for engagement, mistaking conflict for meaning.

This cycle has profound consequences.

Consider the case of journalist Bari Weiss, who resigned from The New York Times after facing continuous ideological attacks from her colleagues. The very outrage culture that she once navigated turned against her, illustrating how those who rely on outrage for validation often become its next target. This is the reality of dependency—eventually, it consumes those who feed it.

True empowerment does not come from outrage. It comes from stepping outside of the cycle, from recognizing that reacting is not the same as influencing, that being offended is not the same as being right, and that real power is found in clarity, not conflict.

The present moment does not demand outrage. It does not require validation through grievance. It only asks: Can you see the illusion for what it is? Can you step away?

Reflection: Building Emotional Autonomy

There is a deep stillness within each person, but it is often drowned out by the noise of perpetual outrage. The reactive mind clings to grievances, believing that its anger is necessary, even righteous. Yet, the moment outrage becomes habitual, it ceases to serve any higher purpose. It no longer responds to injustice—it feeds on itself, demanding more and more until the individual is left depleted, frustrated, and imprisoned by their own reactions.

> *The real cost of outrage addiction is not just emotional depletion but the narrowing of intellectual freedom, where inquiry and dissent are suppressed in favor of rigid, automatic reactions.*

To step out of this cycle is to reclaim emotional autonomy. It is to recognize that outrage is a choice, not an inevitability. The world will always contain conflict, but suffering arises when that conflict is internalized—when it becomes part of personal identity rather than an external event to be witnessed with clarity. If you had to live one full day without engaging in outrage, who would you be? That is where your freedom begins. True resilience is not found in reacting to every perceived slight but in remaining grounded despite them.

Recognizing the Personal Cost of Outrage Addiction

Those who live in a constant state of emotional agitation pay an invisible price. The body remains tense, the mind restless, the emotions fragile. The nervous system, wired for survival, treats every perceived offense as a threat, flooding the bloodstream with cortisol and adrenaline. Studies have shown that chronic outrage correlates with heightened stress, anxiety, and increased risks of depression.[11] The more one engages in outrage, the more the body suffers, yet the mind continues to seek new grievances, unable to rest.

Beyond physical consequences, outrage addiction erodes resilience. A mind conditioned to seek offense becomes brittle, intolerant of disagreement,

---

[11] *Boyd et al., 2020*

hypersensitive to dissent. Instead of growing stronger, it becomes more fragile, needing constant validation. When personal identity is built on opposition—on defining oneself by what one is against rather than what one stands for—it creates an unstable foundation, one easily shaken by differing perspectives.

Intellectual freedom also diminishes. Instead of exploring ideas openly, the outraged mind clings to dogma, rejecting nuance. The ability to learn, to engage with complexity, to listen without judgment—these all suffer when outrage becomes habitual. The greatest cost, then, is not just emotional exhaustion, but the narrowing of awareness itself.

Reflection Questions: *Challenging Emotional Reactivity and Reclaiming Intellectual Freedom*

These questions are designed to help you reflect on the interplay between emotional reactivity and intellectual autonomy. As you consider these, think about how emotional detachment from outrage may open up the possibility for greater mental clarity and freedom.

- Can you identify how your emotional reactivity may limit your intellectual freedom? When you react emotionally to something, do you allow space for questioning, or does your mind shut down in defense of your beliefs? Just as you have the power to disengage emotionally from outrage, can you also disengage from the mental conditioning that demands ideological purity?

- What would it look like to challenge your own reactions—not just emotionally, but intellectually? How can breaking free from outrage addiction enable you to reclaim your freedom of thought?

- How often do you find yourself reacting to things without truly engaging in deeper thought? What would it look like to step back, observe your reaction, and then choose a response that aligns with your deeper values, rather than the emotional pull of immediate reactivity?

"For every minute you remain angry, you give up sixty seconds of peace of mind."

— Ralph Waldo Emerson

Breaking Free from the Cycle of Reaction

Have you noticed how the mind seeks outrage? How, without thinking, the fingers reach for the phone, scrolling through one controversy after another? The mind says, I need to stay informed, but is this really true? Or is it simply an addiction to stimulation, to emotional arousal, to the feeling of being right?

Step back and watch. Observe the impulse before it takes control. The moment before you click, before you react, before you type. What is driving it? Is it clarity, or is it compulsion? If you were truly at peace, would you need to consume more outrage? Would you need to participate in every argument?

> *When the mind no longer reacts but observes, space opens for peace, clarity, and personal freedom—where reactivity gives way to intentional action.*

The mind will resist this awareness. It will say, But I have to engage. I have to respond. This is important. But is it? Or is this just another pull of addiction, another craving mistaken for necessity? The world will go on whether you react or not.

The question is:

- Can you watch without reacting?
- Can you see without being pulled in?

Mindfulness is not about changing what happens outside of you. It is about changing your relationship to it. A thought arises, a news headline flashes, an opinion appears that you disagree with. In that moment, can you observe the space before reaction? The brief pause before the mind labels, judges, and prepares to engage? This is where freedom exists—not in controlling the world, but in not being controlled by it.

Notice how a trigger arises. Perhaps someone says something that offends you. Instantly, the body tenses. The chest tightens. The breath shortens. But what is actually happening? Is there a real threat, or just a thought? And if it is only a thought, why does the body react as though it is in danger?

There is no need to suppress this reaction. Simply observe it. The mind will try to justify its outrage, to explain why it is necessary. But the body tells a different story—it suffers. It holds tension, it carries stress, it remains locked in a cycle of reaction. Can you see this? Can you feel it?

And if you can, why hold onto it?

What if, instead of reacting, you allowed the moment to pass? What if you saw the trigger, acknowledged it, but did not let it take control? What if you no longer needed to prove yourself, to argue, to correct? Imagine the space that would open in your life. Imagine the peace.

Reframing outrage is not about accepting injustice—it is about not becoming enslaved by reactivity. There is a vast difference between responding with wisdom and reacting with compulsion. The latter drains you. The former restores you.

The world will always contain conflict. People will always say things you do not agree with. Events will unfold that seem unfair. But does your suffering help? Does your outrage bring clarity? Or does it only keep you locked in a cycle of agitation?

To reclaim your mind is to reclaim your life.

The question is not whether the world will provoke you. It will. The question is whether you will let it.

And the answer, always, is yours.

Cultivating Resilience & Personal Empowerment Through Detachment

Detachment does not mean indifference. It does not mean you stop caring. It means you stop being consumed. The world will always contain conflict. Opinions will rise and fall. Events will unfold. But can you remain still? Can you see the outrage, feel its pull, and yet not be drawn in? When the mind no longer reacts, a space opens. In that space, there is peace. And in that peace, true power exists.

Resilience grows in proportion to one's ability to step back, to choose response rather than reaction. This is true empowerment—not the fleeting rush of anger, not the illusion of control that outrage provides, but the deep and abiding stability of an undisturbed mind.

Can you observe what outrage does to the body? The tension, the shallowness of breath, the constant need for more? Does it strengthen, or does it deplete? And if it depletes, why hold onto it? Who are you without it? The world will continue— conflict will rise and fall, opinions will shift, events will unfold. But within you, there can be stillness. Not apathy, not passivity, but presence. In presence, there is no compulsion to react. Only clarity. And in that clarity, true power exists.

The greatest illusion of outrage is that it gives power when, in reality, it takes it. It feeds on attention, drains clarity, and leaves the mind restless—always searching for the next conflict to validate its existence.

But there is another way. One that does not require exhaustion, conflict, or the approval of others. Breaking the cycle is not surrender. It is reclaiming what has always been yours—your energy, your clarity, your freedom. The moment you see this, the game ends. Outrage will call. But will you answer?

Outrage Addiction Insight: The Emotional Toll of Outrage Dependency

The mind becomes what it consumes. Repeated exposure to outrage rewires the brain, creating a dependency on emotional arousal. The momentary rush of moral indignation provides a sense of righteousness, but like any addictive cycle, the high is fleeting, and the crash is inevitable.

> *Outrage is a cycle of dependency, where emotional arousal is sought for temporary satisfaction, yet it only leads to an ongoing depletion of energy and clarity.*

Psychological Impact on the Body and Mind

Outrage does not resolve. It only repeats. The body remains tense. The mind, restless. The next conflict always waits. The body remains tense, the breath shallow, the mind unsettled. This is suffering, not strength. To see this clearly is the beginning of freedom.

The mind believes that outrage is power. That to be angry is to be strong. But if this were true, why does it leave you exhausted? Why does it consume rather than restore? There is a hidden dependency here—an attachment not to justice, but to the feeling of being right. The next conflict is always waiting, the next proof that 'they' are wrong. But where does it end? And who suffers? The outrage does not bring resolution, only repetition. To step away is not weakness. It is freedom.[12]

The Paradox Continues: Loss of Power Through Engagement

The paradox is clear: The more outrage is indulged, the less powerful the individual becomes. Emotional reserves deplete. Focus weakens. Relationships

---

[12] *Orben et al., 2020*

suffer. The very act that feels like strength—engaging in constant moral combat—ultimately leads to a profound sense of helplessness and fatigue. The only way to break free is to recognize that outrage is not the source of personal power; it is the thief of it.

"Anger, resentment, and jealousy don't change the heart of others—they only change yours."
— Shannon L. Alder

Outrage Addiction Insight

Why does outrage leave you feeling exhausted yet craving more?

Chronic engagement with outrage leads to repeated cortisol spikes, keeping your body in a state of hyperarousal.[13] Over time, this contributes to emotional exhaustion, anxiety, and depression. Paradoxically, each engagement with outrage also releases dopamine when validated by others, reinforcing the addictive cycle of emotional depletion.[14]

---

[13] *Sapolsky, 2004*
[14] *Sinha, 2008*

Outrage Addiction Insight

Why does outrage contribute to societal division?

Research on social identity theory shows that engaging in tribalistic behavior triggers dopamine release when group affiliation is reinforced.[1] This sense of belonging strengthens in-group loyalty while fostering hostility toward outsiders. The addictive nature of group validation leads to deepened societal polarization and a breakdown of cross-group empathy.[2]

---

[1] *Tajfel & Turner, 1986*
[2] *Brewer, 1999*

Chapter Eight

The Fear of Thought

"Injustice anywhere is a threat to justice everywhere."

— Martin Luther King Jr.

The Silent Weight of Suppression

Free thought cannot survive where fear rules speech. A society that once thrived on debate, curiosity, and exploration now punishes those who question the wrong ideas. Outrage has become the new enforcer, not of truth, but of conformity. What emerges is not a culture of curiosity, but one of enforced agreement, where ideological conformity replaces open dialogue.

Outrage culture does not merely challenge ideas; it seeks to eliminate those who do not conform to its expectations. The result is a society where individuals suppress their true thoughts, not out of conviction, but out of fear. The question is no longer What is true? But What am I allowed to say?

> *Fear does not silence truth—it only buries it beneath the noise of conformity.*

How Outrage Culture Breeds Hostility Toward Free Thought

The impulse to censor is not new. Throughout history, those in power have silenced dissenting voices. But today's outrage culture operates differently—not through legal decrees, but through mass social coercion. People do not fear imprisonment for their words; they fear professional ruin, public humiliation, and social ostracism.

> *Censorship does not need enforcers when the mind learns to suppress itself.*

This climate of fear has reshaped institutions. The New York Times forced editorial page editor James Bennet to resign after he published an op-ed by U.S. Senator Tom Cotton, which, while controversial, fell well within the bounds of public debate.[1] The backlash was not about engaging with the argument—it was about ensuring that it could not be spoken.

When disagreement is treated as dangerous, conversation ceases to be about seeking truth and becomes a test of loyalty. Those who hesitate to conform find themselves on the receiving end of outrage—not because they are wrong, but because they failed to signal the correct position fast enough.

The Shift from Open Discourse to Ideological Orthodoxy

Disagreement was once seen as a natural consequence of human diversity. Now, it is viewed as a moral failing. Societal norms have shifted from encouraging debate to demanding ideological purity. The modern landscape does not allow for uncertainty, for exploration, or for hesitation. One must take a side immediately, or risk being condemned for silence.

Jodi Shaw, a former Smith College employee, resigned after being pressured to accept an ideological framework that categorized individuals solely by race, regardless of their personal experiences.[2] She was not dismissed for incompetence or misconduct—her refusal to participate in what she viewed as ideological coercion made her an outsider.

This is how control operates. It does not always require explicit censorship; it simply makes nonconformity unbearable. People self-censor, not because they are convinced, but because they are exhausted.

---

[1] Grynbaum & Marc, 2020
[2] Shaw, 2021

> *The need to belong binds the mind to illusion.*
> *The willingness to stand alone reveals truth.*

Internalized Suppression: How Fear Becomes Control

When fear polices thought, no external censorship is needed. It is not imposed from above—it is internalized, silent, and absolute.

Fear of exclusion, professional ruin, or public shaming is a more effective tool than censorship. Unlike explicit bans, this suppression is invisible—not enforced, but absorbed. The result is not just silence but a slow, unconscious erosion of independent thought.

> *When thought is dictated by fear, speech is no longer expression—it is performance*

Bret Weinstein, a professor at Evergreen State College, learned this firsthand when he refused to participate in a race-based separation event. His refusal did not spark debate—it triggered protests, threats, and the eventual loss of his job. His punishment was not for being wrong, but for stepping outside the bounds of ideological purity.

The Illusion of Safety Through Consensus

Why does society drift toward ideological conformity? Because the mind equates agreement with security. It assumes that if an idea is widely accepted, it must be correct. But truth does not emerge from consensus; it exists independently of collective approval.

To see through this illusion, one must be willing to observe without immediate judgment. The fear of questioning is not a sign of strength in an idea, but of its fragility. A culture that punishes inquiry is not confident—it is afraid.

The path to intellectual freedom begins not with defiance, but with awareness. When one sees the mechanism of control—when one recognizes the pressure to conform—there is already a distance between the self and the fear. That distance is where choice exists. And in that choice, there is freedom.

> *The moment you observe the fear of speaking, you are no longer controlled by it.*

Self-Reflection: When I hesitate to speak, is it wisdom guiding me—or fear? Do I silence myself because I lack clarity, or because I fear rejection? Am I choosing silence, or has silence been chosen for me?

Intellectual Suppression: The Silent Erosion of Free Thought

A mind conditioned by fear will not speak freely. It will hesitate, censor itself, and retreat into the safety of silence. The moment an individual becomes aware that expressing certain thoughts may result in condemnation rather than discussion, the landscape of discourse changes. It is no longer about the pursuit of understanding but about survival within an ideological system.

The suppression of free thought does not announce itself with force. It is quiet, gradual. It takes root when people notice which opinions are met with approval and which invite punishment. Fear settles into the body, and over time, even the impulse to question fades. This is how intellectual suppression flourishes—not through external control, but through the internalization of limits.

> *A mind that seeks certainty cannot find truth. A mind that seeks truth must embrace uncertainty.*

The Culture of Fear in Academia and Public Discourse

Education was once regarded as a space for inquiry, where questioning assumptions was not only allowed but encouraged. Now, universities—places that should be the vanguard of free thought—have become some of the most ideologically rigid environments.

Speakers are disinvited, faculty members are investigated for discussing contentious topics, and students police their own language to avoid social or academic consequences. In 2021, Dorian Abbot, a geophysicist at the University of Chicago, was invited to give a lecture at MIT.[3] The topic? Climate science. But because he had previously criticized diversity, equity, and inclusion policies as a form of discrimination, his invitation was rescinded. His expertise in science became irrelevant; only ideological purity mattered.

This pattern repeats across institutions. Kathleen Stock, a professor of philosophy, was forced to resign from the University of Sussex after students and faculty protested her views on gender identity. Her work was rooted in logic and analysis, but analysis itself had become dangerous.[4]

In an environment where deviation from the dominant ideology results in professional ruin, free thought does not survive. People may still hold unspoken doubts, but they will not articulate them. Fear has done its work.

Institutional Conformity: Enforcing Ideological Compliance

When an idea is no longer subject to debate, it ceases to function as an idea. It becomes dogma. Universities, corporations, and media organizations now operate as enforcers of ideological compliance. The expectation is not just silence on controversial issues but active participation in a narrative that cannot be questioned.

Corporate workplaces have adopted mandatory ideological training programs that demand agreement rather than discussion. Employees at Coca-Cola were instructed to "be less white" in a diversity training program that framed an entire racial identity as problematic.[5] The message was clear: not only must employees comply, but they must also internalize the ideology.

Media institutions shape public perception by controlling which voices are amplified and which are erased. In 2020, The New York Times published an op-ed by Senator Tom Cotton advocating for military intervention in response to nationwide riots. The article, though controversial, reflected a real position held by many Americans. But after staff members protested, the editorial page editor was forced to resign, and the paper issued an apology.[6] The marketplace of ideas had been replaced with a demand for ideological allegiance.

Where conformity is required, thinking ceases. Institutions that once existed

---

[3] *Abbot, 2021*
[4] *Stock, 2021*
[5] *Reilly, 2021*
[6] *Grynbaum & Marc, 2020*

to foster creativity and challenge assumptions have instead become vehicles for reinforcing an ideological status quo.

> *"The health of a democratic society may be measured by the quality of functions performed by private citizens."*
> *— Alexis de Tocqueville*

The Fear of Deviating from the Group

A society that discourages disagreement does not need laws to enforce its rules—social pressure is enough. The fear of exclusion, of professional loss, of public shaming is more effective than censorship. The punishment for deviation is not prison, but exile.

In 2018, David Shor, a data analyst for a progressive firm, was fired after tweeting a study that suggested peaceful protest movements were more effective than violent ones in achieving political change. The study was by a black Princeton professor, but that did not matter. His tweet was labeled "racist," and he lost his job.[7] His intent was irrelevant. His impact—how his words were perceived—was all that mattered.

This is the psychological mechanism at play: the fear of being cast out of the tribe. Humans are social creatures, and exclusion is felt as deeply as physical pain. When society demands ideological purity, individuals learn to suppress independent thought not because they have changed their beliefs, but because they understand the consequences of speaking them.

> *The need for approval is the quietest form of imprisonment.*

The Awakening from Fear

The suppression of thought is not imposed by external force alone. It is sustained by internal fear. To step out of this fear requires awareness—awareness of the mechanism of control, awareness of the tendency to self-censor.

A mind that can observe its own fear without being ruled by it is already free. When one notices the moment of hesitation before speaking, the tightening of the

---

[7] Mounk, 2020

chest, the question—Is it safe to say this?—there is a choice. That choice is where freedom begins.

Self-Reflection: "*Am I truly free in my thinking, or do I unknowingly follow the patterns of collective belief? If I could think without fear of consequence, how would my thoughts change?*"

The Cultural Consequences of Groupthink

When a society rewards conformity and punishes deviation, it does not merely suppress certain opinions—it reshapes how people think. Thought is no longer an exploration but a performance. Ideas are not examined but recited. Those who step outside the boundaries of permissible discourse are not debated but removed. In this climate, independent thought becomes a liability, creativity is suffocated, and trust in institutions erodes.

A mind that fears questioning will cease to question. And when entire societies surrender to groupthink, something deeper is lost—our ability to trust what we know to be true

The Death of Critical Thinking

A society that trades critical thinking for ideological conformity does not stand still—it drifts. Without the ability to question ideas, people are not just uninformed; they are easily led. Instead of evaluating reality based on reason and evidence, emotional reasoning takes its place. What feels true is accepted as truth.

This shift is visible in how public debates are conducted. Disagreements are no longer resolved through rational discourse but through emotional appeals and personal attacks. The act of questioning dominant narratives is framed as harmful, making discussion impossible. In 2017, Bret Weinstein, a biology professor at Evergreen State College, challenged a mandatory "Day of Absence" in which white students and faculty were asked to leave campus. He argued that coerced racial segregation, even if well-intended, was counterproductive. Instead of engaging with his argument, protesters labeled him a racist and demanded his resignation. The college administration, fearing backlash, failed to protect his right to speak. Weinstein was eventually forced to resign.[8]

This is what happens when emotional reasoning replaces critical thinking. The

---

[8] Weinstein 2017

capacity to analyze, question, and debate is no longer valued. Instead, ideological purity becomes the measure of legitimacy. Without critical thinking, society is left with unquestioned dogma.

> *Conformity does not create unity. It creates quiet desperation.*

The Stifling of Innovation and Creativity

Creativity thrives in an environment of intellectual freedom. When that freedom is replaced with fear—fear of being misunderstood, fear of backlash, fear of punishment—expression withers. Artists, scientists, and thinkers retreat from bold exploration and instead produce work that aligns with safe, acceptable viewpoints.

History is filled with moments when cultural rigidity stifled progress. Under Soviet rule, the state dictated truth; today, society does. The mechanism has changed, but the outcome is the same—truth is sacrificed to ideology.

In 2021, J.K. Rowling, the author of Harry Potter, expressed concerns about gender identity ideology and its impact on women's rights. The response was not a reasoned debate but a coordinated effort to denounce her as transphobic. Publishers distanced themselves, organizations removed her name, and death threats followed. [9]

The message was clear: certain viewpoints are not just controversial but unacceptable.

This climate does not encourage creative or intellectual exploration. It conditions people to self-censor before they even begin. Innovation does not come from those who fear consequences—it comes from those willing to challenge prevailing assumptions.

The Erosion of Public Trust in Institutions

Look around—when institutions demand obedience instead of truth, trust erodes. And when trust is gone, what remains?

News organizations that once prided themselves on impartiality have abandoned objectivity in favor of narrative-driven journalism. In 2020, The New York Times faced internal rebellion after publishing an op-ed by Senator Tom

---

[9] (Rowling, 2021)

Cotton advocating for military intervention in response to nationwide riots. Journalists within the organization argued that publishing the piece itself was an act of violence. The paper ultimately apologized, and the editor responsible resigned.[10]

When institutions demonstrate that they are unwilling to tolerate ideological diversity, they alienate the public. Polls show that trust in mainstream media is at historic lows, with many Americans believing news organizations actively mislead the public.[11] Universities, once the bastion of open inquiry, are now seen as politically biased, leading many students to self-censor in the classroom.[12]

A society cannot function without institutions the public trusts. Yet, when those institutions appear to serve ideology rather than truth, skepticism becomes the default response.

> *The moment you see the mechanism of control, it begins to lose its grip.*

Breaking the Cycle

Groupthink thrives in environments where fear silences curiosity. The way out is not through force, but through awareness. The moment an individual becomes conscious of their hesitation to speak, to question, to explore, they have already taken the first step toward intellectual freedom.

Awakening from groupthink does not mean rejecting all prevailing opinions. It means refusing to accept them without thought. It means engaging with ideas not as mandates but as possibilities to be examined. A mind that is aware of its conditioning can begin to free itself. And a free mind, unburdened by fear, is capable of independent thought once again.

Self-Reflection: "When everyone around me agrees, do I assume the matter is settled? Or do I have the courage to ask—what if we are all mistaken?

---

[10] Grynbaum & Marc, 2020
[11] Edelman Trust Barometer, 2022
[12] Knight Foundation, 2021

The Suppression of Dissent in Public and Private Life

A mind constrained by fear is a mind in conflict. When the external world dictates which thoughts may be spoken and which must be buried, a fracture occurs. The natural flow of expression is halted, replaced by hesitation and self-censorship. The need for acceptance overrides the desire for truth.

The consequence is not just silence, but a deep-seated unease. The weight of unspoken words, the suppression of questions, and the avoidance of difficult conversations create an internal pressure. Over time, this pressure manifests as stress, anxiety, and detachment. People become strangers to themselves, performing agreement rather than engaging in honest discourse.

The Impact on Individual Autonomy

When expression is conditioned by fear, authenticity is lost. In academic and professional spaces, individuals weigh their words carefully, not for clarity, but for safety. The pressure to conform is subtle but unrelenting. The hesitation before speaking, the calculation of consequences, the avoidance of topics that might provoke—these are the quiet markers of control.

Surveys conducted in recent years reveal that many individuals in academic and corporate environments now avoid discussing their views openly, anticipating social or professional backlash.[13] This reluctance is not limited to workplaces. Friendships, family gatherings, and even casual interactions are now navigated with caution. Words are filtered, not for accuracy, but for acceptability.

In this climate, the erosion of personal autonomy is inevitable. The freedom to express is replaced by the compulsion to conform. Silence becomes self-preservation. And yet, this silence carries its own cost. Suppressed thoughts do not disappear; they linger, creating an internal conflict between what is known and what is permitted to be spoken.

Social Fragmentation: Communities Divided by Ideological Purity

A society that demands ideological purity fractures into rigid factions. The search for agreement turns into a demand for allegiance. Individuals are categorized not by their character, but by their compliance with prevailing narratives.

---

[13] *Cato Institute, 2020*

The consequence is isolation. Those who express even mild dissent risk social exile. The space for nuance shrinks. Friendships dissolve over ideological divides. Professional relationships are severed over perceived infractions. A 2021 report on social cohesion found that ideological polarization had deepened significantly, with individuals increasingly reluctant to associate with those who hold differing views.[14]

This fragmentation is particularly evident in digital spaces. Social media algorithms reinforce division by curating content that aligns with existing beliefs. Users are presented not with a broad spectrum of perspectives, but with an echo of their own thoughts. The illusion of consensus is maintained by the exclusion of dissenting voices.

The result is not unity, but division. Individuals withdraw into ideological enclaves where conformity is rewarded, and deviation is punished. The collective mind narrows, conditioned to see opposition not as a perspective to be understood, but as a threat to be eliminated.

Case Studies: Societal Backlash Against Intellectual Suppression

History repeatedly demonstrates that the suppression of dissent is unsustainable. Attempts to enforce ideological conformity do not create consensus—they provoke resistance. The human mind, when restricted, searches for release.

The Harper's Letter: A Cultural Fault Line in Intellectual Freedom

In 2020, Harper's Magazine published an open letter signed by a diverse group of intellectuals, defending free discourse over ideological coercion. It took no political stance; it simply affirmed that intellectual freedom is foundational to a functioning society.

The response was immediate—and revealing. Some signatories faced professional consequences. Others, fearing backlash, publicly retracted their support. The letter was not debated on its merits but condemned as reactionary, even dangerous. The message was clear: defending free speech itself had become controversial.

The pattern is consistent across institutions. Compare this to Bret Weinstein's experience at Evergreen State College or David Shor's firing for sharing an academic study. The mechanism is the same: challenging the dominant ideology—

---

[14] Pew Research Center, 2021

no matter how rational or well-intended—is not met with engagement but with elimination.

When even calls for open discourse are framed as threats, what remains? A culture that no longer values truth—only conformity.

Silencing Science: Public Health Dissent and Its Repercussions

A similar backlash unfolded in 2021 when a group of high-profile scientists challenged dominant narratives on public health policies. Their research was legitimate, their concerns data-driven—yet their work was met with suppression. Some were censured by their institutions; others were deplatformed entirely.

Yet within a year, many of their warnings proved accurate. This reinforces a crucial lesson: silencing dissent does not eliminate truth—it only delays its recognition.[15]

Lessons from History: The Persistence of Underground Thought

The suppression of ideas is not a new phenomenon—nor is the failure of suppression as a long-term strategy. In the 1980s, underground publications in Eastern Europe played a crucial role in challenging authoritarian narratives. Writers, journalists, and intellectuals—barred from mainstream media—distributed ideas through samizdat networks, bypassing state-controlled censors. Despite the risks, these efforts laid the groundwork for larger movements that eventually led to political change.[16]

The patterns repeat today. When speech is policed, thought does not disappear—it moves elsewhere. When public discourse is restricted, it finds new channels. The suppression of dissent never leads to lasting conformity—it only fuels the search for alternative spaces where truth can be spoken without fear.

Self-Reflection: "*Have I ever abandoned my own insight to preserve harmony? What have I left unspoken—not because it was wrong, but because it was unwelcome? If you could relive the moment without fear, what would you have said?*

---

[15] *Brownstone Institute, 2021*
[16] *Applebaum, 2012*

Reflection: Rebuilding a Culture of Intellectual Courage

A mind that is free does not seek validation. It does not demand agreement, nor does it fear contradiction. It observes, it questions, and it remains open. But when a society conditions individuals to avoid disagreement—when the mere act of questioning is seen as a threat—intellectual courage withers. The space for independent thought collapses, and with it, the foundation of a free and evolving culture.

To rebuild this space, awareness must precede action. The recognition that discourse has been hijacked by fear, that disagreement is treated as hostility, is the first step toward reclaiming the ability to think, speak, and engage without constraint. Intellectual courage is not about confrontation; it is about presence— the ability to stand firmly in inquiry without being swept into the tide of collective outrage.

> *The silence beneath suppression is not absence; it is where freedom begins.*

The Importance of Protecting Intellectual Diversity

Intellectual diversity is not merely a societal good; it is a necessity for growth. No civilization has ever thrived on the uniformity of thought. Creativity, innovation, and moral progress arise not from consensus, but from the willingness to challenge assumptions.

Throughout history, societies that have enforced ideological conformity have stagnated. The cultural revolutions of the 20th century, from Maoist China to Stalinist Russia, demonstrated the dangers of silencing intellectual dissent. Literature, science, and philosophy suffered not because truth ceased to exist, but because the freedom to explore it was denied. Even in democratic societies, the suppression of contrarian perspectives leads not to stability, but to decline in critical thought and cultural richness.[17]

Safeguarding intellectual diversity is not about promoting conflict; it is about ensuring the vitality of discourse. When individuals fear dissent, they stop thinking

---

[17] *Sowell, 1987*

deeply. When they fear expression, they stop engaging with new ideas. And when they fear speaking, the entire society suffers from an impoverishment of wisdom.

Strategies for Fostering Open, Respectful Debate

Rebuilding intellectual courage begins with small, personal choices. The ability to engage without hostility, to listen without judgment, and to speak without fear is cultivated in daily interactions.

Encouraging Curiosity Over Outrage

Outrage is reactive; curiosity is expansive. When an individual encounters a perspective that contradicts their own, there is a moment of choice. One can react with defensiveness, reinforcing ideological rigidity, or one can become curious. What experiences led this person to their belief? What do they see that I do not? What do I believe that I have never questioned? This shift—from reactivity to inquiry—creates the conditions for meaningful dialogue.

Creating Spaces for Dialogue That Allow for Disagreement Without Hostility

Conversation is not a battleground. It is an opportunity to explore. In a culture dominated by ideological purity tests, where deviation is met with condemnation, disagreement becomes synonymous with enmity. This is an illusion. A thriving discourse does not require uniformity, but rather the ability to disagree without personal animosity. This is evident in societies where debate is still valued—where conflicting views are seen not as a threat, but as an opportunity for refinement.[18]

Social structures, from universities to workplaces to public platforms, must move away from punitive reactions to ideological divergence. Instead of fostering environments where individuals are conditioned to silence themselves, institutions must actively cultivate settings where discussion is encouraged, and disagreement is welcomed as a sign of engagement rather than defiance.

The Role of Dissent in Strengthening Democratic Discourse

A culture that fears dissent cannot remain free. The right to question is the foundation upon which democracy stands. When individuals relinquish this right—whether out of fear, exhaustion, or social pressure—they surrender not just personal autonomy, but the collective ability to adapt, improve, and refine ideas.

Throughout history, the most profound shifts in social consciousness have

---

[18] *Haidt, 2018*

emerged from those who challenged the dominant narrative. The abolition of slavery, the expansion of civil rights, the advancement of science—these movements were all initially unpopular. They thrived because individuals, despite being vilified, refused to accept consensus as truth.[19]

In modern discourse, the suppression of dissent is often justified under the guise of social harmony. But forced harmony is not peace. It is suppression in disguise. True democratic discourse requires the tension of conflicting perspectives, the willingness to tolerate discomfort, and the recognition that no ideology—no matter how righteous it appears—can remain unchallenged without becoming oppressive.

> *The world will always present reasons to be outraged. Awareness reveals a deeper truth: real strength is found not in rigid certainty, but in the ability to question without fear.*

Returning to Presence

The need to be right is an extension of the ego. It resists challenge, fearing the dissolution of identity that comes with uncertainty. But truth is not something to be possessed—it is something to be approached, endlessly refined through inquiry, not defended through certainty.

The world will always present reasons to be outraged. There will always be voices demanding ideological obedience, insisting that certainty is strength. But awareness reveals a deeper truth: real strength is found not in rigid certainty, but in the ability to question without fear.

To resist the pull of conditioned outrage is not to disengage from the world but to engage with it more deeply—through clarity rather than compulsion.

This is the first step toward breaking free from groupthink: noticing the impulse to conform before it becomes action. When one sees the mechanism of social conditioning—the silent pressure to obey, to signal, to belong—it loosens its grip.

From this awareness, action can follow—not as a reflexive reaction, but as a conscious, deliberate choice.

---

[19] *Loury, 2021*

Self-Reflection: *"Do I seek validation, or do I seek truth? Can I welcome disagreement as an opportunity for growth rather than as a threat to my identity? Can I listen without the urge to defend?"*

Outrage Addiction Insight: The Psychological Cost of Groupthink

The need for belonging is deeply embedded in the human psyche. Social acceptance once meant survival; rejection meant isolation, vulnerability, and even death. In modern society, this primal instinct persists, but instead of seeking safety in physical numbers, individuals seek safety in ideological conformity. When outrage culture dominates, groupthink takes hold—not as an intellectual choice, but as a subconscious survival mechanism.

Neuroscientific research shows that social exclusion triggers the same neural pathways as physical pain.[20] The brain interprets rejection—whether from a tribe, a workplace, or an online community—as a direct threat. This leads individuals to self-censor, suppressing independent thought to avoid social punishment. The cycle deepens as outrage becomes a marker of loyalty, signaling adherence to the collective mindset.

The dopamine-driven nature of social media reinforces this pattern. Each public display of outrage, each performative act of moral signaling, is met with immediate social validation—likes, retweets, and supportive comments. This feedback loop conditions individuals to prioritize ideological compliance over intellectual integrity.[21] Those who stray, even slightly, face the psychological distress of ostracization, leading many to remain silent or adopt positions they do not truly hold.

The long-term cost of this dynamic is profound. Fear of dissent stifles creativity, weakens problem-solving, and erodes resilience. Societies that embrace ideological conformity at the expense of open discourse experience intellectual stagnation, where critical thinking is replaced by emotional reactivity.[22] In the individual, the suppression of true beliefs leads to inner turmoil—cognitive dissonance, chronic stress, and emotional exhaustion.

Breaking free from groupthink requires a conscious shift from reactivity to presence. Real security is not found in agreement but in awareness. A mind that no longer seeks approval is a mind that is free. The mind that is not bound by the need for approval is free to observe, question, and evolve. In this space, real clarity—and real freedom—becomes possible.

---

[20] *Eisenberger, 2003*
[21] *Tufekci, 2017*
[22] *Sunstein, 2003*

Chapter Nine

The Economics of Offense

"It is difficult to get a man to understand something when his salary depends upon his not understanding it."

— Upton Sinclair

Outrage as a Lucrative Industry

There is a moment when the world pauses, not because of silence, but because of noise—the noise of outrage. It fills every space, moves through every channel, and feeds on every impulse of reaction. Yet beneath this storm of indignation, something quieter is at play: a marketplace. A transaction. Outrage has become an industry, not merely an emotion.

The Business of Outrage

What was once a spontaneous response to injustice has now been refined into a commodity. Outrage is measured, analyzed, and repackaged as engagement. It moves through news cycles, headlines, and digital platforms, not as a call to awareness but as a currency exchanged for profit. The more intense the reaction, the greater its value. The more divisive the issue, the more lucrative its appeal.

The mind, once caught in this current, believes it is participating in something meaningful. But participation is not the goal—it is retention. The longer a person remains within the cycle of outrage, the more valuable they become to those who monetize their emotions. The digital economy thrives on attention, and nothing holds attention more than anger.

> *Outrage feels like moral action, but in the hands of corporations, it is merely currency—traded, repackaged, and resold in a market where engagement is profit.*

The Transformation of Social Activism into Commerce

Activism, in its purest form, arises from stillness—an awareness of suffering, a recognition of injustice, and a deep, unwavering commitment to change. But when activism becomes entangled with commerce, its nature shifts. It is no longer about transformation but about optics. A movement is no longer measured by the depth of its impact but by the breadth of its reach.

Corporations, sensing the profitability of aligning with popular causes, do not support movements—they brand them. They take the language of justice and merge it with slogans, turning protest into product placement. A movement ceases to be a force of change when it becomes a marketing campaign. It no longer asks for sacrifice or courage but for clicks, shares, and consumer loyalty.

There is a moment when one can feel this shift, when the energy of true activism is replaced by performance. The outrage remains, but the purpose dissolves. What is left is an echo—a repetition of slogans, a manufactured anger that fuels engagement but rarely leads to resolution.

The Profit Motive Behind Manufactured Moral Panic

The mind, when gripped by fear, does not question. It reacts. It seeks safety in conformity and validation in collective outrage. Corporations and media institutions have learned to harness this, turning moral panic into a business model. The pattern is predictable: identify a controversy, amplify its most extreme voices, present a simplified narrative, and ensure continued escalation.

The result is a world where fear and outrage are not just reactions but products—sold in advertisements, embedded in algorithms, and distributed through carefully curated messaging. What is presented as urgent and immediate is often a distraction, not from reality, but from presence. The mind, overwhelmed by a manufactured crisis, loses sight of what is real.

The question, then, is not whether outrage is justified. It often is. The question is whether it is being used. When the energy of human concern is redirected into an industry of profit, something profound is lost. Awareness is replaced by reaction.

Wisdom is replaced by impulse. In this cycle, suffering does not end—it is simply repackaged and resold.

The moment one sees outrage for what it is—an impulse fueled by collective conditioning, an addiction disguised as moral urgency—something shifts. The mind, once gripped by the need to react, begins to loosen its hold. A spaciousness emerges. It is subtle at first, like stepping out of a crowded room into open air. The tension, the mental noise that seemed inseparable from existence, is revealed as optional. Without the compulsion to engage in the outrage economy, what remains is a presence so simple that it was overlooked all along. The need to assert, to defend, to correct dissipates, and in its absence, there is only stillness. Not the stillness of passivity but the quiet power of clarity. In this space, outrage no longer holds the mind captive; it is seen for what it is—just another movement on the surface of awareness, passing like a ripple on water. And when one no longer identifies with the ripple, the ocean remains.

> *The moment you see outrage for what it is—a product designed to capture your attention—you begin to step out of its grip. Without reaction, there is only clarity.*

Outrage as Industry: The Corporate Exploitation of Division

The Business Model of Outrage

Outrage is not accidental. It is not merely a byproduct of passionate discourse or an inevitable response to injustice. It has become a commodity—an engine of profit, meticulously engineered and sustained. What was once an emotional reaction has been refined into a product, bought and sold in a marketplace of constant agitation.

Modern corporations do not create outrage from nothing; they amplify it. The structures that sustain outrage—media outlets, social platforms, advertising models—thrive on engagement. And engagement in the digital economy is most easily sustained through conflict. Each click, each share, and each moment spent lingering over a provocative headline is recorded, analyzed, and converted into revenue. This is the hidden economy of modern outrage: a system that turns human reactivity into financial gain.

> *Outrage is no longer just an emotional response; it is a business model. And like any industry, it thrives not on resolution, but on perpetual crisis*

Advertising revenue fuels this cycle. Algorithms designed to maximize engagement do not differentiate between content that informs and content that incites. They simply promote whatever holds attention the longest. And nothing holds attention like anger. The more inflammatory the claim, the more likely it is to spread. The more division a message sows, the more valuable it becomes. It is a cycle that feeds itself, an engine that runs on the fuel of human reaction.

The irony is that while outrage appears to be about justice, about righteousness, about standing for something meaningful, it is often nothing more than a tool, a mechanism designed not to enlighten but to ensnare. The moment one sees this, the machinery behind the outrage is revealed. The spell begins to break.

The Rise of Corporate Moral Posturing

Corporations do not take moral positions. They take profitable ones. A brand does not care whether an idea is true or false, whether a movement is just or misguided. It cares whether it sells. The language of morality has become the language of commerce, and in this transformation, something essential is lost.

In this new landscape, virtue is a marketing strategy. A corporation aligns itself with a cause, not out of conviction but calculation. Slogans are crafted not for sincerity but for shareability. Statements of solidarity are issued, not in pursuit of change but in pursuit of visibility. And yet, beneath the surface, nothing shifts. The mechanisms of exploitation remain intact, only now wrapped in the language of activism.

But something deeper is happening. The more corporations participate in this performance, the more the nature of moral discourse itself is altered. Activism, once a pursuit of truth and transformation, is now filtered through the lens of public relations. Issues of great significance are reduced to branding exercises. The outrage, though real in the hearts of many, is repackaged and resold, stripped of its original intention.

To see this clearly is to step outside the cycle. When morality is used as a tool for profit, it ceases to be morality. It becomes performance. And true transformation—the kind that is not driven by profit but by presence—begins only when one ceases to be hypnotized by the theater of corporate virtue.

Media Manipulation: Outrage for Ratings

The media does not report reality as it is. It shapes reality as it is consumed. The landscape of modern information is not designed to inform but to provoke. The language is precise, the imagery curated, and the emotional triggers deliberately chosen. And why? Because attention is currency.

News cycles are not dictated by significance but by engagement. A story that inflames will be prioritized over a story that enlightens. A narrative that divides will be amplified over one that reconciles. This is not because media organizations conspire to mislead but because they are built to survive. And in the modern era, survival is tied to outrage.

Yet, beyond the headlines, beyond the relentless stream of controversy, there is stillness. A moment where one steps back and sees the pattern. The provocation, the reaction, the escalation. Again and again. Each story, each outrage, each demand for immediate emotional response. But when one does not react—when one does not feed the cycle—something remarkable happens. The weight of the outrage dissolves. The urgency fades. And what remains is clarity.

> *Corporations do not take moral positions; they take profitable ones. And in the economy of outrage, sincerity is the first casualty.*

True awareness does not emerge from consuming more information but from recognizing the way information is used. To see how outrage is manufactured is to step outside its grip. And when that happens, the mind is no longer caught in the machinery of reaction. It returns to stillness. And in that stillness, the possibility of real change—free from manipulation, free from profit-driven agendas—can begin.

Activism for Profit: The Commercialization of Social Justice

Monetizing Movements

There was a time when activism arose from a place of deep conviction. It was not an accessory, not a slogan, not a carefully curated image. It was raw, unpolished, and often uncomfortable. It disrupted, not for attention, but for transformation. Today, the landscape has shifted. What was once an organic force for change has become a product, something packaged and sold in the marketplace of identity and belonging.

Movements, once the heartbeat of social transformation, are now commodities. Their symbols, their language, and their very essence are absorbed into the machinery of commerce, repurposed to generate profit. A cause is no longer simply a cause—it is a brand. And with branding comes dilution. The power of genuine activism lies in its ability to challenge, to upend, to demand reflection. But in the hands of corporations, these sharp edges are softened, repackaged into something digestible, something palatable, something that does not unsettle, but affirms.

When a movement becomes a marketing tool, it loses its soul. It is no longer about the truth of the message, but the appeal of the aesthetic. It is no longer about difficult conversations, but seamless integration into a company's brand identity. And so, the movement, once a fire that burned for justice, is reduced to a flickering LED on the storefront of corporate virtue.

Awareness changes everything. To see this process unfolding is to step outside its grasp. A moment of stillness is enough to recognize that true activism cannot be bought, nor can it be sold. It exists only in presence, in action untainted by self-interest, in the quiet certainty of those who seek truth over applause.

> *When a movement is repackaged for mass consumption, its sharp edges are dulled, its urgency diluted, and its truth commodified.*

Outrage Merchandising: Selling the Message

Anger is profitable. Righteousness is marketable. The language of justice, once spoken in the streets, now appears on limited-edition hoodies, coffee mugs, and sleek digital advertisements. And beneath it all, the unspoken transaction: moral identity in exchange for a purchase.

The modern marketplace has learned to manufacture belonging. To wear the right slogan is to signal the right beliefs. To carry the right tote bag is to align with the right cause. In this way, action is no longer required—only consumption. And consumption, unlike true transformation, demands nothing of the individual beyond the transaction itself.

This is how meaning is lost. When an idea becomes a product, its depth is flattened. The suffering, the struggle, the complexity behind a movement cannot be condensed into a tagline, yet that is precisely what happens. In the rush to commodify, the spirit of the message is sacrificed for its marketability.

And so, a paradox emerges: the more a movement is embraced by corporations, the less radical it becomes. The more it is packaged for easy consumption, the less it challenges the status quo. This is not by accident. A genuine movement, one that asks hard questions and resists being co-opted, is dangerous to the very structures that corporations exist to uphold.

But awareness changes the nature of participation. When outrage is stripped of its commercial appeal, when it is no longer a style but a stance, a space opens for something real. A shift from performance to presence. A shift from branding to being. This is the movement that cannot be bought.

Nonprofits and NGOs: Profit Motives in Advocacy

Not all who speak of change seek it. Not all who claim to fight injustice stand apart from the machinery that perpetuates it. Within the world of advocacy and nonprofit organizations, an uncomfortable truth emerges: outrage is a currency, and for some, it is more valuable sustained than resolved.

The nonprofit sector, once regarded as a space of selfless service, has in many cases become indistinguishable from the industries it was created to counter. The structures are the same—hierarchies, branding, marketing strategies designed to elicit emotional responses. The difference is in the product being sold. Instead of goods, it is urgency. Instead of services, it is awareness. And yet, awareness, when endlessly cycled through without transformation, becomes an industry in itself.

A movement that is solved is a movement that no longer generates revenue. A crisis resolved is a crisis that no longer compels donations. And so, the incentive exists to keep the struggle visible, to keep the urgency alive, to keep the story circulating in a way that sustains the organization more than it serves the cause. This is not cynicism; it is simply the nature of a system that, like any other, depends on its own survival.

> *True activism does not require branding. It exists not in performance, but in presence—not in what is proclaimed, but in what is done.*

This is not to say that all advocacy is hollow, nor that all who work within these spaces are complicit. But awareness is required. To see where genuine service ends and where self-preservation begins. To discern whether the action being taken is designed to dismantle or to perpetuate. To recognize that the loudest voices are not always the most sincere.

Beyond the noise, beyond the performances of activism, there is something deeper. A presence that does not need validation, a commitment that does not require branding. That is where true change begins. Not in the market, not in the media, but in the quiet resolve of those who act not for recognition, but because they cannot do otherwise.

The Cost of Corporate-Driven Outrage

Superficial Activism and Public Skepticism

When a cause is reduced to a campaign, when moral conviction is transformed into a marketing strategy, something essential is lost. The energy that once propelled genuine movements forward dissipates, replaced by scripted messaging, empty promises, and gestures designed for optics rather than impact. The result is a slow erosion of trust, not only in the corporations that claim to champion these causes but in the causes themselves.

Consumers recognize insincerity. When a brand proclaims its unwavering commitment to justice one moment, only to be exposed for exploitative labor practices the next, the contradiction is impossible to ignore. When businesses engage in activism not out of genuine concern but as a calculated move to maintain relevance, the movement itself becomes suspect. The backlash that follows is not merely a rejection of corporate hypocrisy but a deeper disillusionment with the entire landscape of social advocacy.

> *In an economy built on outrage, exhaustion is inevitable. The more we consume, the less we feel, until only numbness remains.*

A moment comes when people begin to disengage. Not because they no longer care, but because they have been conditioned to see activism as another performance, another spectacle, another mechanism of control. This is the hidden cost of superficial activism—not just the discrediting of brands but the disillusionment of the public. A culture that no longer believes in the sincerity of change is a culture that drifts into apathy.

Yet beyond this, there is something more real, more alive. A movement that does not rely on approval or mass adoption. A stillness that does not need branding. In the absence of commercial motives, true change emerges, not from a place of performance but from awareness.

Innovation Stifled by Corporate Censorship

Fear constrains creativity. When every idea, every artistic expression, every new initiative must first be filtered through the lens of potential outrage, what remains is not truth but calculation. Corporations, desperate to avoid controversy, impose unspoken rules—certain topics must not be explored, certain perspectives must not be voiced. And so, the environment shifts from one of free expression to one of careful compliance.

This is the subtle grip of control. Not through overt suppression but through the quiet enforcement of self-censorship. Artists, writers, comedians, and thinkers begin to second-guess their instincts. Employees tread carefully, not because they lack ideas but because they fear the consequences of expressing them. The corporate world, once a space of ambition and risk-taking, becomes a landscape of pre-approved narratives.

The consequences are not merely professional. On a deeper level, the act of constant self-monitoring creates an inner fragmentation—a disconnection between what is felt and what is allowed to be expressed. To live in fear of words, of ideas, of perspectives that may be deemed unacceptable, is to live in a state of perpetual anxiety.

But there is a way forward. Not through rebellion or confrontation, but through presence. To see the mechanism of control is to loosen its grip. To recognize the fear is to step beyond it. Creativity, when freed from the burden of external validation, becomes something vast, something uncontainable. It is only in this space that true innovation can arise.

When activism is reduced to a trend, disillusionment follows. The price of corporate virtue-signaling is a culture that stops believing in real change.

Economic Consequences of Outrage Dependency

An economy built on outrage is inherently unstable. Like any addiction, it requires ever-increasing doses to sustain engagement. What was once shocking becomes ordinary, what once generated intense reactions now barely registers. And so, the cycle intensifies—brands and media outlets push further, amplify conflict, manufacture new crises to ensure that attention never wavers.

But outrage, when used as a business model, has a diminishing return. Consumers grow weary. The emotional toll of constant conflict leaves them exhausted, cynical, disengaged. And when outrage is no longer an effective tool for profit, companies must shift yet again, searching for the next strategy to capture attention.

This is the deeper cost—beyond the instability of corporations, beyond the damage to brand reputations. It is the exhaustion of an entire culture, the fraying of social cohesion, the gradual numbing of people who once cared deeply but have been conditioned to see every issue as a product, every movement as a fleeting trend.

"The business of the journalists is to destroy the truth... We are the tools and vassals of rich men behind the scenes. "   *— John Swinton*

Still, awareness dissolves the illusion. When outrage is no longer seen as a necessity, when it is no longer consumed mindlessly, something changes. A different way of being emerges—one that does not react, but observes. One that does not consume, but questions. One that sees through the illusion of urgency and returns to presence. And in that space, true transformation is possible.

Reclaiming Authentic Activism from Corporate Exploitation

Distinguishing Genuine Activism from Commercial Exploitation

True activism arises not from the mind's desire for recognition but from an inner alignment with what is just. It does not seek validation through mass approval, nor does it require a corporate sponsor to affirm its legitimacy. It moves from a deeper place, beyond the pull of consumer culture, beyond the machinery of profit-driven causes.

In the world of commerce, everything is for sale—even conviction, even outrage. What once began as a movement, raw and unfiltered, is soon packaged into campaigns, slogans, and branded merchandise. The fire that once burned from within is dimmed, repurposed for optics, for engagement, for quarterly reports. A cause that becomes a commodity is no longer a cause—it is a product.

> *To withdraw from the outrage economy is not indifference—it is the first step toward clarity. Change does not begin in reaction, but in awareness.*

To see this clearly is to awaken from the illusion. Not with anger, not with resistance, but with awareness. The distinction between genuine activism and its commercial counterpart becomes evident the moment one stops reacting and starts observing. Authentic action does not need an audience. It does not require an orchestrated social media campaign. It simply is.

Encouraging Businesses to Support Meaningful Change

The presence of corporate interests in activism does not mean that businesses are incapable of supporting meaningful change. But change cannot be dictated by marketing trends or public sentiment alone. If a company truly seeks to support a cause, it must be willing to do so beyond the moments when it is profitable, beyond the seasons when it is popular.

Supporting real change is not an act of branding but of being. It requires action that extends beyond the surface—fair wages instead of token philanthropy, ethical sourcing instead of symbolic partnerships. A corporation that aligns itself with justice must embody that justice in its practices, in its treatment of employees, in the way it operates when no one is watching.

Anything less is performance. And performance, no matter how polished, is always fleeting. The public, though momentarily engaged, eventually senses the hollowness behind empty gestures. A corporation that truly seeks to make an impact does not need to advertise its virtue—it simply integrates it into its way of being.

> When morality is used as a marketing tool, it ceases to be morality. Only when it is free from profit does it have the power to transform.

Consumer Responsibility: Disengaging from Profit-Driven Outrage Cycles

A cycle cannot continue without participation. When outrage is manufactured for profit, its survival depends on one thing: engagement. It needs the click, the share, the reaction. Without these, it dissolves.

This is the great shift—not a battle against the system, but a quiet refusal to be drawn in. The realization that one does not need to respond to every provocation, that attention is a currency more valuable than money, that presence is the only space where clarity can arise.

To disengage does not mean to become indifferent. On the contrary, it means to act from awareness rather than compulsion. It means to recognize when a cause is being used as bait, when moral outrage is being repackaged into a transaction. It means to move in alignment with truth, not with trends.

And so, the question is no longer "How do we fight this?" but rather "How do we stop feeding it?" The answer is simple: by withdrawing attention from what is false and returning it to what is real. By stepping out of the storm of reaction and into the stillness that has always been present. From that space, activism is no longer performance. It is no longer driven by ego, by fear, by division. It is simply an expression of what is, unclouded and free.

> "Advertising is the art of convincing people to spend money they don't have for something they don't need."
> — Will Rogers

Chapter Ten

Emotional Resilience in a Hyper-Offended World

"Between stimulus and response, there is a space. In that space is our power to choose our response."

— Viktor E. Frankl

The Importance of Emotional Resilience in an Age of Outrage

Understanding Emotional Resilience

Emotional resilience is not what most believe it to be. It is not about strength in the way the world defines it—resisting, enduring, or overcoming. It is about no longer deriving one's sense of self from the shifting tides of external circumstances. To be resilient is not to fight against offense, nor is it to manage it. It is to step beyond it entirely—to awaken to a state of being that is no longer defined by reaction. It is not a form of detachment that turns away from life, nor is it indifference. It is the ability to remain present, aware, and unmoved by the pull of conditioned reactivity.

In a culture where outrage has become the default mode of engagement, emotional resilience is an act of quiet defiance. To be resilient is to no longer be a puppet of external forces—to no longer be pulled into the endless cycle of reaction and counter-reaction. It is the ability to see an inflammatory headline, a provocative statement, or an offensive remark without losing oneself in the emotion it triggers.

True resilience does not mean suppressing emotions. Suppression is another form of resistance, and resistance always strengthens what it seeks to avoid. Rather, resilience is the ability to experience an emotion fully while remaining aware that you are not the emotion.

> *Emotional resilience is not about fighting against offense, nor is it about managing it. It is the realization that offense only has power when it is believed.*

When offense arises, resilience allows one to observe it without becoming consumed by it. Without this inner strength, there is only reaction—habitual, compulsive, and automatic. And where there is no choice, there is no freedom.

True strength is not in resisting the tide, but in realizing you are the ocean beneath it.

The Difference Between Genuine Offense and Conditioned Outrage

Not all offense is the same. Some offenses point to real injustice, genuine harm, or necessary change. But much of what is called offense today is something else entirely. It is not an organic response to the present moment but a conditioned reaction—a learned behavior shaped by the environment, the media, and social reinforcement.

When a person feels outrage, they assume the feeling itself is proof of its validity. If I feel it, it must be true. But emotions, like thoughts, arise from conditioning. And like any habit, outrage becomes addictive—feeding on validation, social reinforcement, and the illusion of control. It does not emerge from presence but from a script that has been rehearsed over time.

A simple test reveals the difference between genuine offense and conditioned outrage. If an offense is genuine, it carries a stillness beneath it. There is clarity, and within that clarity, there is the space to respond thoughtfully. But when outrage is conditioned, it is restless. It demands immediate action, immediate condemnation, immediate retaliation. It is fueled not by presence but by an unexamined mental pattern, a script being played out over and over again.

When offense arises, pause. Is this reaction coming from direct experience, or is it inherited? Is it arising from presence, or is it something I have been taught to feel?

In this pause, there is freedom.

Reclaiming Control Over Emotional Responses

To be free from the cycle of conditioned outrage is not to ignore the world. It is to see it with greater clarity. And in that clarity, true action—action that is not reactive, not compulsive, but deeply aligned with reality—becomes possible.

Awareness begins not in grand gestures, but in the subtle noticing of how reactivity plays out in daily life. A moment of offense arises—not as an independent force, but as the echo of countless influences: social narratives, past experiences, and unconscious mental patterns. To cultivate resilience is not to deny these influences, but to see them clearly. When seen, their hold begins to loosen. From this space of observation, practical steps emerge—not as rigid techniques, but as pathways to deeper presence. When a person is exposed to outrage repeatedly, it begins to shape their perception of reality. They do not simply see events; they see them through the lens of offense. The mind becomes hyper-vigilant, scanning for the next reason to be outraged, the next reason to affirm its existing beliefs.

But the moment one steps back and witnesses this pattern—truly sees it—something changes. There is a shift from identification to awareness. The emotion still arises, but now it is observed. And in this observation, its power diminishes.

> *You are not the reaction. You are the awareness in which the reaction arises. In this seeing, its grip begins to loosen.*

When reaction dissolves, what remains is a quiet spaciousness—an opening where presence takes the place of struggle. In this space, offense is no longer something to overcome, but something to witness. And in this witnessing, the need to react begins to fall away.

Emotional resilience is not the absence of emotion but the space in which emotion arises without overwhelming presence.

To reclaim your emotional autonomy is to reclaim your freedom. And to be free is to no longer be at the mercy of the world's provocations.

Once you witness the pattern of reaction, the next step is to reclaim your ability to choose. This choice is the foundation of true resilience.

∞∞∞∞

In every moment, there is a choice. To react, or to be still. To be pulled into outrage, or to remain grounded in presence. To follow the conditioned mind, or to awaken to a deeper reality.

Most people do not realize that they have this choice. They believe their emotions dictate their responses, not realizing that emotions, too, are shaped by unconscious patterns.

But the moment awareness enters, the cycle begins to break. And when the cycle breaks, so does its hold on you. In that moment, you realize: you were never bound—only unaware of your freedom.

Recognizing Genuine Offense vs. Conditioned Outrage

The Nature of Reflexive Reactions

There is a moment, almost imperceptible, before reaction. It is a silent space, one that disappears when the mind is fully identified with the emotion of the moment. The more conditioned the response, the smaller that space becomes—until there is no longer a choice, only reaction. The world speaks, and the body flinches. A comment is made, and anger surges. Something is read, and indignation takes hold. This is the state of unconsciousness—where offense is not experienced but expected.

What we often call "being offended" is, at its root, a conditioned response. The mind, accustomed to certain thought patterns, reacts predictably when those patterns are disrupted. Over time, the reaction becomes habitual, even involuntary. It is no longer questioned. It simply happens. But this is not the same as awareness.

In an age where outrage is cultivated like a commodity, exposure to provocative content is relentless. Social media, news cycles, and even conversations have become arenas where emotional activation is the currency. The more deeply entangled one becomes in these external stimuli, the more reflexive the reactions become. Thought is no longer examined; it is assumed. Emotion is no longer witnessed; it is owned. The identity fuses with the reaction, until the offense feels personal, absolute, and non-negotiable.

Yet, something happens when the reaction is observed rather than indulged. A space appears. And in that space, a question arises: Was this reaction inevitable, or was it chosen? If it was inevitable, then there is no freedom—only programming. But if it was chosen, then there is another possibility: It does not have to be this way.

The recognition of this space is the beginning of awareness. And awareness is the undoing of unconscious reaction.

> *There is a moment before reaction—a silent space, easily missed. In that space, there is freedom. Awareness begins there.*

Identifying Deep-Seated Emotional Triggers

The mind is quick to assume that offense is caused by external events. A statement, a headline, an image—these are seen as the source of distress. But what if they are merely the surface? What if the real trigger lies elsewhere, buried beneath layers of past experiences and unresolved emotions?

Once we recognize the habitual nature of outrage, a deeper question emerges: Why does it arise so easily in some and not others? Why do certain words, actions, or ideas trigger such strong emotions while others pass unnoticed? The answer lies not in the event itself, but in the unseen emotional imprints it awakens. These imprints—traces of past experiences, insecurities, and unresolved wounds— operate beneath conscious awareness, yet they dictate how we respond to the present moment. When we mistake a triggered emotion for objective reality, we remain trapped in its cycle.

Often, the answer is not found in the present moment but in the past. A belief that was challenged in childhood. A feeling of powerlessness once experienced. A deeply held insecurity. A pattern of rejection, of being misunderstood, of not being heard. These emotional imprints remain, unseen yet deeply felt, influencing every interaction. And when something in the present moment touches them—even slightly—it is not just the present moment that reacts, but the entire past behind it.

> *What offends you is not the event itself, but what it touches within you. The pain is not new—it is only being revealed.*

This is why different people respond so differently to the same event. One person shrugs off a comment, while another feels deeply wounded. One person sees a headline and moves on, while another feels compelled to react, to engage, to fight. It is not the event itself that holds power—it is what it touches within.

Offense is not always false. But without awareness, one cannot discern between an authentic wound and the echo of past conditioning.

The moment this is understood, something shifts. The reaction may still arise, but now it is seen. And in that seeing, the unconscious compulsion to react begins to dissolve.

Breaking the Cycle of Automatic Outrage

Reaction is a trap disguised as urgency. Mistaking movement for meaning, the mind remains caught in the cycle it seeks to escape.

The way out is not through suppression but through presence—an awareness that allows you to observe without immediately reacting. When presence deepens, the habitual need to defend or retaliate weakens. The space between stimulus and response expands, creating room for conscious choice instead of compulsive reaction. This shift is not theoretical; it is a lived experience, cultivated through small, daily acts of awareness.

The next time offense arises, pause. Not to deny the feeling, but to witness it. Where in the body is this feeling appearing? Is it in the chest? The stomach? Is there tightness, heat, restlessness? By bringing attention to the physical sensation of offense rather than immediately engaging with the thoughts surrounding it, the identification with the reaction weakens.

Then, a question: What is the thought behind this emotion?

Every emotional reaction has a thought fueling it. It may sound like:

- This is wrong. This is unacceptable.
- I am being attacked.
- They are the problem.
- I need to respond, or I am complicit.

These thoughts feel absolute in the moment. But are they true? Not just subjectively true, but fundamentally, beyond thought itself—are they true?

Or is this simply the mind repeating a familiar narrative?

To pause is not to become passive. It is to disengage from unconsciousness. When there is no longer automatic identification with offense, there is choice. One may still choose to respond—but now, it is a response, not a reaction. One may still feel strongly—but now, it is observed rather than being mistaken for the self.

The world does not need more outrage. It does not need more reaction. It needs the stillness that sees both without being consumed by either. Presence begins where reaction ends.

ooooo

This is not about dismissing offense or silencing the voice that speaks against injustice. It is about recognizing the difference between reactive outrage and conscious awareness. One is compulsive; the other is clear. One seeks conflict; the other seeks truth.

To live free from the cycle of conditioned outrage is not to ignore the world but to see it with greater clarity. And in that clarity, action—true action—becomes possible.

Building Emotional Resilience: Practical Strategies

The mind is conditioned to react. It moves swiftly, attaching itself to offense, to opinion, to the impulse to correct, to argue, to resist. This is the nature of unconscious identification: to mistake every passing thought, every rising emotion, for reality. But what happens when you pause? What happens when, instead of reacting, you become aware?

This is the beginning of emotional resilience.

Resilience is not about force, nor is it about suppressing emotion. It is about seeing clearly, recognizing the patterns that pull you into suffering, and stepping out of them. Without this awareness, offense becomes a habit, a reflexive loop that repeats itself endlessly. With awareness, that loop is interrupted. And in its place, there is space—space to respond rather than react, space to observe without becoming lost in the emotion.

The following practices are not techniques in the conventional sense. They are invitations to awareness. If applied with presence, they do not simply change behavior—they transform how you experience the world.

"Do not teach your children never to be angry; teach them how to be angry."   — *Lyman Abbott*

Trigger Awareness Exercise: Naming the Reaction

Each moment of offense is an opportunity to wake up. But most do not see it this way. They become lost in the emotion, believing the intensity of their reaction justifies itself.

Awareness breaks this cycle. The next time offense arises, pause. Instead of immediately reacting, observe the reaction itself.

- What exactly triggered me?

- Why do I feel this way?

- Is this offense truly about the situation in front of me, or does it stem from something deeper—an insecurity, an unresolved emotion, a conditioned belief?

At first, the mind will resist. It will demand validation. It will want to argue, to justify its response. But stay with the observation. Write it down. Capture the thoughts, the emotions, the physical sensations. Not to analyze them, but simply to see them for what they are.

In this act of naming, something shifts. The reaction loses its grip. It is seen not as an absolute truth, but as a passing wave in awareness. And with this, a new possibility emerges: the choice to engage, or the choice to let go.

This is the beginning of freedom.

When a trigger arises, pause. Feel the reaction, observe it, but do not become it. The moment you witness it, you are free.

Boundary-Setting Techniques: Protect Your Emotional Space

Not every battle is worth fighting. Not every opinion needs a response. Yet the mind, conditioned by external stimulation, seeks conflict. It feels compelled to engage, to correct, to defend itself against every perceived offense. But what if you simply chose not to participate?

Protecting your emotional space is not avoidance. It is clarity. It is the realization that engagement is not always necessary, that reaction is not always required. It is stepping away from the unconscious pull of outrage and choosing instead to remain present.

> *Most people seek to control the world so they no longer feel disturbed. But true freedom comes not from control, but from no longer being controlled.*

Practical ways to establish this boundary:

1. Limit exposure to outrage-heavy media. Be mindful of what you consume. The mind absorbs patterns. If you constantly feed it outrage, it will seek it out.

2. Avoid debates on platforms that discourage real dialogue. Social media rewards quick reactions, not deep thought. Recognize when a conversation serves no real purpose.

3. Practice assertive disengagement. If a conversation is pulling you into unconscious reaction, say:

> – "I choose not to engage with this right now."

> – "I understand your perspective, but I don't feel the need to argue."

It is not weakness to disengage. It is strength. The ability to walk away from unnecessary conflict is the mark of emotional mastery.

Disengagement Through Mindfulness: The Power of the Pause

There is a brief space between stimulus and response. Most do not see it. They move from trigger to reaction without awareness. But in that small space, there is freedom.

Mindfulness is the practice of expanding that space. It is learning to rest in awareness instead of being pulled into reaction. The next time you feel the familiar rush of offense, try this:

1. Take three deep breaths. Breathe in deeply, hold for a moment, and exhale slowly. Feel the air moving through your body. Let this physical sensation ground you.

2. Count backward from five. This short delay interrupts the habitual response, allowing space for awareness to emerge.

3. Reframe the thought with neutrality. Instead of immediately judging, shift the language in your mind:

- Instead of "This is unacceptable," try "That is their perspective."
- Instead of "I need to say something," try "Does this need my energy?"

By pausing, you reclaim choice. You are no longer at the mercy of conditioned reactions. Instead, you remain rooted in presence, able to respond with clarity or let go entirely.

Over time, this practice becomes second nature. And what once provoked an immediate reaction begins to pass like clouds in the sky—seen, acknowledged, but no longer clung to.

ooooo

Emotional resilience is not something to be acquired. It is something to be uncovered. It is already within you, beneath the layers of conditioning, beneath the habitual reactions that have been learned over time.

When you are fully present, there is no need to defend, no need to prove, no need to be outraged. There is simply clarity. And in clarity, there is peace.

Freedom is not found in controlling the world but in no longer being controlled by it.

Emotional Mastery: From Reaction to Reflection

The mind, conditioned by habit and external influence, often seeks its sense of self in reaction. It believes power lies in asserting itself, in being heard, in responding to every perceived slight. But is this true power, or merely the continuation of an unconscious pattern? But if you look closely, you will see the paradox: the more you react, the more powerless you feel. Each reaction feeds the cycle, draining energy, creating more turmoil, leading to yet another reaction.

Notice the impulse to react. Feel the subtle pull of identification with offense. The mind grasps at it, seeking affirmation, seeking validation. But in observing this grasping, something else appears—a spaciousness in which the reaction no longer seems so inevitable.

The conditioned mind fears stillness. It survives on movement, on conflict, on identification with thought. Reaction affirms its existence. And so, without awareness, you become pulled into its storm—compulsively defending, attacking, correcting—mistaking this endless engagement for control.

But real power is not in reaction. It is in presence. It is in seeing the reaction arise, but not becoming it.

When you recognize this, something shifts. The space between stimulus and response opens. And within that space, there is freedom.

Learning to Choose Your Reactions

A moment arises. A comment, a post, a situation unfolds that does not align with what you believe should be. The body tenses. The mind speeds up, preparing a defense, constructing an argument, replaying the offense.

Notice this.

Before you react, pause. Not as suppression, but as awareness. Observe the urge to respond, to justify, to correct. Observe the thoughts forming, the emotions swelling. And ask:

Who is reacting?

If you are aware of the reaction, then you are not the reaction. The mind is speaking, but you are the one listening. The emotion is present, but you are the space in which it arises.

Can you see the difference?

A reaction, when seen, begins to lose its grip. It no longer carries the same urgency. You may still choose to respond—but now, it is a conscious response, not an automatic reflex.

This is mastery. Not the suppression of thought, not the denial of emotion, but the realization that you do not have to follow them.

> *The need to react is the mind's attempt to affirm itself. But you do not need to affirm what has always been.*

Reframing Offense as an Opportunity for Growth

What does offense reveal? If you meet it with presence rather than resistance, what does it show you? Does it expose an assumption you have mistaken for truth?

Does it highlight an identity you feel the need to defend? Instead of reacting, simply witness the response. There is no need to analyze or justify—just observe. In that space, something deeper begins to emerge: the recognition that what is being challenged is not who you are but what you have believed yourself to be

Perhaps the reaction is not about the other person at all. Perhaps it is a reflection of something deeper—an unexamined belief, a hidden insecurity, an unresolved wound.

Every offense is an opportunity. It invites you to turn inward, to explore the reaction itself. Instead of engaging outward, fighting the external, you can pause and ask:

- Why does this affect me so strongly?

- What belief is being threatened?

- Is the discomfort pointing to something I need to see within myself?

A simple practice: Each time offense arises, try this—before reacting, take a breath and ask, 'What if this moment is here to reveal something, not attack something? What belief am I clinging to? What happens if I loosen my grip?' Sit with the question. Do not rush to answer. Simply hold space for the discomfort, allowing awareness to reveal what the mind might have overlooked. In this stillness, reaction begins to dissolve, and understanding emerges.

Then, after a few moments, write down one sentence: 'I am offended because...' and complete the thought. Pause. Read what you wrote. Now ask, 'Is this absolutely true? Or is it a story my mind is telling?' This small act of witnessing begins to unravel the compulsion to react.

Notice how the ego resists this. It wants the source of offense to be out there, to remain external. Because if it is external, then the problem is with the world, not with the self.

But when you begin to use offense as a mirror, something shifts. What once seemed personal becomes impersonal. The charge of the reaction fades. The trigger loses its power.

Suddenly, offense is no longer a burden—it is a teacher. And when offense is no longer a burden, you become free.

The Strength in Silence

The mind may equate silence with weakness, mistaking stillness for passivity. It believes strength lies in words, in defense, in being right. But notice what happens when reaction falls away. What remains is not weakness, but clarity. Not passivity, but presence.

But real power does not need to be proven.

True silence—the kind that arises from awareness, not avoidance—is the highest form of strength. When you no longer feel the need to react, when you no longer need to prove anything, you step into something deeper than victory.

> When reaction falls away, what remains is not weakness but clarity. Not passivity, but presence.

You step into peace.

To walk away is not surrender. It is liberation. It means you are no longer controlled by external forces. You have reclaimed your energy. You have chosen stillness over struggle.

The world may not understand this. It may mistake disengagement for apathy, silence for weakness. But that is only because the world does not yet recognize the power of stillness.

In stillness, the noise of the world loses its grip. And in that stillness, you find something far greater than the need to be right. You find the vast, open sky—the part of you that has always been free.

> "Resilience is accepting your new reality, even if it's less good than the one you had before."
> — Elizabeth Edwards

Outrage Addiction Insight

Why is it so difficult to let go of being offended?

Neuroscience suggests that feelings of moral outrage trigger dopamine release, creating a temporary sense of control and validation.[1] This emotional high becomes addictive, encouraging repeated engagement in offense-driven reactions. Breaking this cycle requires interrupting the dopamine loop through practices that promote mindfulness and emotional regulation.[2]

---

[1] *Rothschild & Keefer, 2017*
[2] *Tang, Hölzel, & Posner, 2015*

Outrage Addiction Insight

Why does performative compassion feel so rewarding?

Neuroscientific studies show that acts of empathy trigger the brain's reward circuitry, particularly when those acts are publicly acknowledged.[3] This validation releases dopamine, reinforcing a cycle where the social reward of being seen as compassionate can become more satisfying than genuine emotional connection.[4]

---

[3] *Zaki & Ochsner, 2012*
[4] *Cikara, Bruneau, & Saxe, 2011*

Reclaiming Empathy and Compassion

"Too often we underestimate the power of a touch, a smile, a kind word... all of which have the potential to turn a life around."
— Leo Buscaglia

Rediscovering the True Nature of Empathy

The word "empathy" has lost its stillness. It has become entangled with the noise of the world, twisted into something performative, something to be displayed rather than lived. In a culture that thrives on validation, empathy is no longer an internal experience—it has become an external performance.

True empathy does not seek recognition. It does not posture, does not demand applause. It is quiet, intimate, and deeply human. It does not rush to be seen as compassionate; it simply is. But modern culture has obscured this simplicity. The mind, conditioned by societal expectation, has turned empathy into a tool of self-identification—something to signal, something to showcase, something to prove.

Yet real empathy arises in the absence of self. It is not about you. It does not exist to validate your virtue, to affirm your moral superiority, or to broadcast your goodness. It is not something to wield, but something to be. It exists only in presence, in the stillness of connection.

The Distortion of Empathy in Modern Culture

When empathy is no longer an act of connection but a display of moral alignment, it loses its essence. The impulse to appear empathetic often overrides the actual experience of empathy itself. The mind crafts an image—a statement, a post, a reaction—that signals care while bypassing the vulnerability that true empathy requires.

This is why modern culture rewards outrage on behalf of others more than quiet, unseen acts of compassion. It is easier to be perceived as caring than to actually care. The former requires only performance; the latter requires presence.

Empathy has become currency in the social economy, where its value is measured in visibility. But this is not the same as genuine concern. The moment empathy becomes about the self—about being 'on the right side,' about receiving approval—it ceases to be empathy at all. It becomes something else: performance.

The Difference Between Authentic Compassion and Virtue Signaling

True empathy does not seek validation. It does not announce itself, demand recognition, or require an audience. It does not need to be seen—it only needs to be felt. But in a world where moral visibility is mistaken for moral virtue, empathy is often performed rather than lived.

Virtue signaling, by contrast, is concern with an audience. It is the projection of empathy, not its embodiment. It is the need to be seen as caring rather than the silent act of caring itself.

Authentic compassion is humble. It is patient. It does not rush to prove itself. It listens. It is not concerned with appearing right; it is concerned with understanding.

Virtue signaling, however, is impatient. It is reactive. It must be declared, often loudly, so that it is not mistaken for silence. But true empathy does not need to declare itself. It does not attach itself to an identity or a cause. It simply meets another person, without agenda, without expectation, without self.

The Power of Presence Over Performance

Empathy is not found in grand gestures. It is found in presence. In listening without interruption. In sitting with another's pain without trying to fix it, without rushing to be the hero in their story.

The mind, when unconscious, believes it must always do something. It must solve, correct, intervene. But true empathy is not about doing. It is about being. To simply be with another person in their experience is the highest form of compassion.

When empathy is stripped of performance, when it is no longer about the self, it becomes an opening. A space where true connection arises. In that space, there is no need to be perceived as good, no need to be right, no need to control the narrative. There is only presence.

This is the path back to true empathy—not as something to display, but as something to embody. Not as an identity, but as a way of being.

True Empathy vs. Performed Empathy

Empathy is not a performance. It is not something to display, nor is it something to prove. It arises naturally, without force, in the space of deep listening and genuine connection. And yet, modern culture has turned empathy into a spectacle—something to be announced, something to be seen.

The mind, conditioned by the world, has learned to equate visibility with virtue. To be perceived as good is more important than to be good. This is the shift that has taken place—where empathy, once an unspoken movement of the heart, has been transformed into an instrument of self-affirmation. But real empathy does not seek validation. It does not perform, posture, or demand recognition. It simply is.

Defining Authentic Empathy

True empathy is the ability to be with another's experience without needing to make it about yourself. It is the willingness to feel what another feels—not as a means to enhance your own identity, but as an act of pure connection.

The mind, when unconscious, is self-referential. It listens only to respond, only to affirm its own sense of self. But true empathy does not impose itself. It does not rush to fix, to correct, to be the savior in someone else's experience. It listens. It holds space. It does not say, I understand because I have felt the same. It simply allows the other person to be seen, to be heard, without needing to insert itself into the narrative.

This is why true empathy requires humility. To be truly present with another person, one must let go of the need to be right, the need to be validated, the need to be seen as compassionate. There is no need to prove anything. Empathy flows when the self is absent.

The Allure of Performed Empathy

Visibility is now mistaken for virtue. To be seen as compassionate has become more important than to be compassionate. But real connection exists beyond recognition—silent, unseen, real.

When empathy is performed, it becomes a tool for self-image rather than connection. It is not about the person who is suffering; it is about the one who wishes to be seen as caring. The mind crafts statements, takes positions, offers outrage—not as a reflection of deep feeling, but as a means of self-elevation.

This is why social media has become the perfect stage for performative concern. In an instant, one can publicly align with a cause, express outrage, or offer support—not through action, but through words alone. And yet, when empathy is about signaling, it is empty. It does not transform, does not heal, does not connect. It only reinforces the illusion of moral superiority.

Examples of performative empathy:

– The hashtag activist who proclaims solidarity online but does nothing to engage with those suffering in real life.

– The public shaming disguised as concern, where someone calls attention to another's wrongdoing—not to help them grow, but to display their own virtue.

– The outrage cycle, where a person reacts intensely to a situation they have no true connection to, simply because it aligns with the identity they wish to project.

True empathy is not about appearing good. It is about being present—a presence that cannot be quantified or publicly affirmed, because it exists in silence, in unseen moments, in the willingness to truly listen.

Recognizing Performative Concern in Yourself and Others

It is easy to recognize performative empathy in others, but more challenging to see it within ourselves. The ego does not like to admit when its motives are impure. But if you pause—if you become deeply present—you can observe when your concern is genuine and when it is tied to self-image.

Ask yourself:

– Is my empathy quiet, or do I feel the need to announce it?

– Am I listening to truly understand, or to affirm my own beliefs?

– Does my concern lead to action, or is it satisfied with appearance?

Empathy that requires an audience is not empathy at all. It is another form of seeking, another way the mind attempts to fortify itself. But when empathy is real, it is enough simply to feel. No announcement is necessary. No approval is needed.

The shift is subtle but profound. When concern is no longer tied to the self, it becomes something else entirely. It becomes compassion, free of agenda, free of performance. It becomes love in its purest form—silent, unwavering, without need for recognition.

This is true empathy. And it is only found in presence.

"Compassion is not a relationship between the healer and the wounded. It's a relationship between equals."
— Pema Chödrön

The Psychology of Compassion Fatigue and Superficial Empathy

Empathy, in its truest form, is a quiet and natural response to human suffering. It does not demand attention, nor does it seek validation. It simply exists—spontaneous, effortless, and real. But in a world saturated with constant calls for outrage and performative displays of concern, empathy has become something else. It has been overstimulated, overexposed, and ultimately exhausted.

There is a cost to living in a state of perpetual empathy—one that many do not recognize until they feel its weight. The exhaustion, the numbness, the growing inability to care as deeply as before. This is compassion fatigue, the silent burnout of a world that never stops demanding emotional engagement.

The Burden of Constant Empathy Exposure

The mind is not designed to process endless suffering. In earlier times, empathy was a personal experience—an intimate connection with those close to us. It was not something broadcast daily, nor was it something expected to be given indiscriminately to every cause, every crisis, every voice calling for attention.

But now, the demand is relentless. A 24-hour cycle of outrage and suffering streams across screens, each tragedy competing for emotional engagement. The mind, overwhelmed, cannot distinguish between what is urgent and what is simply noise. And so, empathy, once a profound and sacred response, becomes dull.

The signs of compassion fatigue are subtle:

– Irritability and frustration toward issues that once evoked deep concern.

– Emotional numbness—a sense of detachment from suffering, not because it doesn't matter, but because the mind can no longer sustain the weight.

– Guilt—for not caring enough, for not reacting strongly enough, for feeling the need to turn away.

This is not a failure of morality. It is a failure of balance. The mind, exposed to too much, protects itself the only way it knows how—by shutting down.

Superficial Empathy as an Emotional Defense

When genuine empathy becomes overwhelming, the mind finds a way to cope. It shifts into performance—a surface-level engagement that does not require true vulnerability. It becomes easier to share, to retweet, to announce support rather than to feel deeply.

Superficial empathy mimics connection but asks nothing of the heart. It allows one to appear compassionate, to align with the collective emotional current, while keeping true feelings at a safe distance.

This is why outrage-driven empathy often feels hollow. It is reactive, not reflective. It does not arise from presence, from stillness, but from pressure. The pressure to care. The pressure to be seen caring. The pressure to align with whatever emotional response is currently expected.

This form of empathy is exhausting not because it is deep, but because it is constant. When empathy is forced, when it is performed, when it is expected at all times—it becomes a burden, not a gift.

Rebuilding Capacity for Genuine Compassion

Real empathy cannot be sustained through force. It arises naturally when there is space—space to breathe, space to be present, space to step away from the noise and reconnect with what is real.

To restore the ability to feel deeply, one must learn to step back. To set boundaries—not out of indifference, but out of wisdom.

Practices to prevent empathy burnout:

– Intentional disengagement – Allowing space from constant exposure to outrage-driven content, creating time for stillness and reflection.

– Selective attention – Recognizing that not every call for emotional reaction requires engagement. Learning to distinguish between true connection and emotional manipulation.

– Grounding in real presence – Engaging in face-to-face conversations, where empathy is not performative but deeply human.

– Letting go of guilt – Accepting that one cannot care about everything, and that selective, meaningful engagement is more powerful than empty displays of concern.

When empathy is rooted in presence, it does not drain. It does not exhaust. It does not require performance. It simply is.

The world does not need more performative concern. It needs people who are fully present.

Cultivating Genuine Empathy: Practical Strategies

True empathy does not come from the mind. It is not an intellectual exercise, nor is it a performance. It arises in the stillness of presence, where no agenda exists—only the openness to experience another's reality without resistance or self-interest. But in a world that conditions people to react rather than listen, to project rather than understand, empathy must often be relearned

These practices are not about acquiring a skill but about remembering what was always there. They guide awareness back to the space where connection is effortless, where the need for validation dissolves, and where presence replaces performance.

1. Active Listening Exercise: The Five-Minute Rule

The mind is rarely silent when another person speaks. It prepares responses, judges words, and constructs its own narrative before the other has even finished speaking. This is not listening; this is waiting for the chance to respond.

To listen is to surrender that impulse—to give another the gift of undivided presence.

The practice:

- The next time you are in conversation, commit to five minutes of uninterrupted listening.

- Focus entirely on the other person's words. Notice when the mind wants to judge, compare, or prepare a response—and let that go.

- When they finish, reflect back what you heard without adding opinions, solutions, or advice.

- Observe the shift in connection. Notice how deep presence alone is enough.

The outcome:

Deep connection is not built on the need to fix, to agree, or to be right. It is built on the simple act of being fully there. When you remove the compulsion to insert yourself into another's experience, what remains is something rare: real understanding.

2. Compassion vs. Validation Journal

Empathy becomes distorted when it is entangled with the need to be seen as compassionate. It becomes less about the other and more about proving something—to oneself or to the world. This need is subtle, yet it shapes the way support is offered.

The practice:

At the end of each day, reflect on one interaction where you offered support. Ask:

- Was I offering genuine compassion, or was I seeking validation for being "good" or "moral"?

- Did my response help the other person, or did it primarily serve my need for recognition?

Write down your observations. Be honest. No judgment—only awareness.

The outcome:

Over time, patterns emerge. You begin to see when empathy is unconditional and when it is intertwined with self-image. And in seeing, you release. The need to prove yourself fades, leaving only the purest form of connection—one that is not about you at all.

3. Forgiveness Framework: The Three-Step Process

Unforgiveness is a barrier to true empathy. When the mind clings to grievances, it cannot fully meet another with an open heart. Forgiveness is not about excusing harm or denying pain. It is about freeing yourself from the weight of carrying it.

The practice:

> – Acknowledge the offense – Write down the event and how it made you feel. Name the emotions without resistance.
>
> – Release the need for retribution – Ask yourself, "What would forgiving this person release within me?"
>
> – Reframe the experience – Reflect on what the situation taught you about your own resilience, values, and capacity for growth.

The outcome:

When forgiveness is no longer about the other person—when it becomes an act of inner peace—its power is realized. It is not a gift to them. It is a release for you.

Empathy does not need to be cultivated. It already exists beneath the noise of the mind. These practices are simply reminders, gentle ways to return to the space where genuine connection is effortless.

In presence, there is no need to prove, no need to perform, no need to hold on. There is only awareness.

And in that awareness, empathy flows.

Reflection and Action: Rediscovering True Compassion

Empathy is not a thought. It is not an action. It is a space—an openness that allows another's experience to exist without interference. But to reach this space, the mind must quiet. The habitual patterns of judgment, analysis, and the need to respond must dissolve.

In modern life, empathy is often mistaken for agreement. To understand someone does not mean to endorse their viewpoint, nor does it require resistance. True empathy exists in the space between reaction and validation.

It is an invitation: I see you. I hear you.

Not I will fix you or I will prove myself through you. Simply, I am here.

These final practices are not tasks to be completed. They are reminders—ways of returning to presence, of allowing connection to emerge naturally.

"Empathy is seeing with the eyes of another, listening with the ears of another, and feeling with the heart of another." — Alfred Adler

We'd Love to Hear From You!

Thank you so much for reading this book-it means the world to me. If you found it helpful, inspiring, or just enjoyable, would you take a moment to leave a review? Your feedback not only helps others but also keeps me motivated to create more valuable content for you.

Here's how you can leave a review:

1. Scan the QR code on this page to go directly to the author's page.

2. Or, visit your Amazon Orders page, find this book, and click "Write a Product Review."

**Your kind words make a big difference.
Thank you for your support!**

Chapter Twelve

Cultivating Intellectual Freedom

"The mind, once stretched by a new idea, never returns to its original dimensions."

— Ralph Waldo Emerson

The Power of Independent Thought

The mind is shaped by what it consumes. Every headline, every conversation, every belief held tightly or loosely—each contributes to the landscape of thought. But how often do you question what you believe? How often do you notice the silent hand of social conditioning guiding your opinions?

Independent thought is not about rebellion, nor is it about contrarianism for its own sake. It is about seeing clearly, without distortion, without the pull of collective identity shaping your perception before you have even had the chance to observe.

Many believe they think for themselves, yet their thoughts are echoes. Repeated phrases, secondhand outrage, the collective hum of accepted truths—all absorbed and repeated without reflection. To reclaim intellectual freedom is to become aware of this process.

> *Most thoughts are not your own. They are echoes—repeated patterns absorbed unconsciously. To think freely is not to add more thoughts, but to become aware of them.*

What Is Intellectual Freedom?

The ability to think independently does not mean arriving at conclusions in isolation. It is not the rejection of influence, nor the dismissal of wisdom from others. Instead, it is the ability to engage with ideas—without fear, without compulsion, without the need for validation or approval.

Intellectual freedom is an internal state. It is the willingness to question not only the world but also yourself. To notice when an opinion arises and ask, Where did this come from? Is it true? It is the ability to hold uncertainty, to resist the pressure to form conclusions too quickly.

The conditioned mind seeks certainty. It wants to belong. It clings to ideology, to group identity, to familiar narratives. And in a world where information is abundant yet filtered, this instinct is constantly reinforced. But true intellectual freedom requires space—room to question, to reconsider, to change.

> *True intelligence does not arise from knowing more, but from questioning what is already known.*

The Modern Threat to Intellectual Freedom

In a world of constant information, the illusion of independent thought is more powerful than ever. Social media algorithms tailor content to reinforce what you already believe. News cycles feed outrage designed to confirm your biases. The need for belonging fosters groupthink, making dissent feel dangerous.

The individual is pressured to align. To express the right opinions. To avoid questioning what should remain unquestioned. The modern world does not demand reflection; it demands reaction. And in reaction, there is no space for clarity.

Outrage culture does not merely punish those who think differently—it erodes the ability to think at all. Fear replaces curiosity. Agreement becomes a requirement. Inquiry is mistaken for disloyalty.

To see this clearly is to step outside of it. To recognize when fear of judgment is shaping your voice. To notice when the need to belong is shaping your conclusions.

To regain intellectual freedom is not to fight against these forces. It is simply to wake up to them.

The Value of Discomfort in Intellectual Growth

There is a moment when an idea unsettles you. Something you read, hear, or encounter contradicts what you believe. The mind tenses. The body resists. A quiet discomfort arises—defensiveness, irritation, even fear.

This is the doorway.

Discomfort is not an enemy. It is the signal of something deeper—an assumption unexamined, a belief held too tightly. The mind wants to resolve it quickly, to dismiss or argue. But if you do not react, if you simply allow the discomfort to be, something shifts.

You see the reaction itself. You notice the ego clinging to certainty. And in that moment, you have a choice: to defend the belief or to explore it.

True intellectual freedom is found here. In the willingness to sit with discomfort, to let it expand your understanding rather than shut it down. This is not about rejecting what you believe. It is about no longer fearing what might change it.

Independent thought does not require agreement. It does not demand certainty. It does not seek approval. It is the willingness to stand alone, not in opposition, but in clarity.

It is the space between reaction and reflection.

And in that space, something powerful emerges—freedom.

The Power of Open Dialogue and Challenging Ideas

A conversation unfolds. Two people stand on opposite sides of an idea, each convinced of their position. Words sharpen. Defenses rise. The mind grasps for certainty, seeking not to understand but to conquer.

This is the state of much of modern discourse—dialogue reduced to competition. The goal is no longer to learn, but to win. To be right. To be seen as right. And so, the walls of understanding close before the first word is truly heard.

But what if the purpose of dialogue was not victory? What if, instead of fortifying our beliefs, we allowed them to be questioned? Not from a place of fear, but of openness? Not as an attack, but as an invitation—to see beyond ourselves?

> *When you listen to defend, you are not listening. When you listen to win, you are not learning. True dialogue begins where the need to be right ends.*

The Necessity of Diverse Perspectives

Truth is not found in isolation. The mind, left unchallenged, becomes stagnant, circling the same familiar conclusions, mistaking repetition for truth. Intellectual diversity is not a threat to clarity—it is the very condition that allows it to arise.

When you encounter a perspective that contradicts your own, what happens? The body tenses. The mind immediately begins to construct a counterargument. There is resistance, a reflexive tightening, as if identity itself is under attack.

But this resistance is not a sign of truth. It is simply habit. The conditioned mind clings to certainty, not because it is correct, but because it is comfortable.

To engage with opposing viewpoints does not mean agreeing with them. It means allowing them to exist, without the immediate impulse to defend or destroy. It means asking, What can this teach me?

True understanding arises when there is space. Space to hear, to reflect, to entertain the possibility that what you believe is incomplete. When you resist this space, you do not protect truth—you shield yourself from it.

The Fear of Intellectual Discomfort

There is a moment when an idea unsettles you. It does not align with what you know. It contradicts the narrative you have accepted. It introduces uncertainty, and with it, discomfort.

This discomfort is not the enemy. It is the threshold.

The mind avoids discomfort because it sees it as a threat. But in reality, discomfort is the signpost of growth. If you only engage with ideas that affirm what you already believe, you are not learning—you are reinforcing.

> *An idea that unsettles you is not an enemy. It is an invitation—to expand beyond what you thought you knew.*

Cognitive dissonance arises when reality does not match belief. The unconscious reaction is to dismiss, to discredit, to cling harder to what is familiar. But another path exists:

To pause.

To notice the reaction without becoming lost in it. To ask, Why does this idea provoke me?

It is not the idea itself that is painful. It is the resistance to seeing beyond what you know. When you stop resisting, the discomfort transforms. It becomes an opening, not a threat.

Reframing Intellectual Conflict as Growth

What if disagreement was not an obstacle, but a teacher?

In every clash of ideas, there is an opportunity—to see more, to understand more, to loosen the grip of certainty that binds the mind. When you shift from a mindset of winning to one of curiosity, conflict ceases to be a battleground. It becomes a space of transformation.

To engage in true dialogue requires presence. It means listening, not with the intent to reply, but with the intent to understand. It means recognizing when the impulse to defend arises, and choosing, instead, to remain open.

Growth is not found in the familiar. It is found at the edges, where discomfort meets awareness. The choice is always yours: to retreat into certainty, or to step into the unknown, where real learning begins.

When you no longer need to be right, you are free to see. And in seeing, you expand.

> *"I disapprove of what you say, but I will defend to*
> *the death your right to say it."* — *Evelyn Beatrice Hall*

The Psychological Barriers to Intellectual Freedom

The mind clings to the familiar. It seeks what feels safe, what reinforces identity, what confirms what it already believes to be true. This is not because the truth has been fully seen, but because the ego fears uncertainty. In a world where certainty is prized and agreement is rewarded, the greatest challenge is not in defending our beliefs, but in questioning them.

The walls of intellectual confinement are rarely imposed by force. More often, they are built by the mind itself—subtle, invisible, reinforced by the need for belonging, by the fear of discomfort, by the deep desire to be right. And so, the prison is mistaken for shelter.

> *The greatest prison is not built of walls, but of certainty. To cling to fixed beliefs is to mistake familiarity for truth.*

To step beyond these walls is to step into openness. But openness requires courage—the courage to see beyond one's own conditioned perspective, the willingness to sit with discomfort, and the strength to endure the loneliness that can accompany independent thought.

Confirmation Bias: The Comfort of Agreement

The mind seeks patterns, not truth. It looks for confirmation, for echoes of its own thoughts, for evidence that supports what is already known. It does not do this consciously, but instinctively, filtering out what does not fit, dismissing what threatens its sense of certainty.

This is the illusion of knowledge. It is not that the information we consume is false, but that it is incomplete. The mind gravitates toward agreement, not because it is wise, but because it is comfortable. And in comfort, there is no expansion.

The danger is subtle. The more one surrounds themselves with agreement, the less one questions. The less one questions, the more certain they become. And the more certain they become, the more resistant they are to anything that challenges them.

But truth does not exist in a vacuum of agreement. It arises only in the presence of contradiction. To see reality clearly, one must be willing to step beyond the echo chamber of their own thoughts. They must ask:

- Do I seek understanding, or do I seek validation?

- Am I truly engaging with ideas, or am I defending an identity?

- When confronted with something that contradicts my beliefs, do I listen, or do I react?

Intellectual freedom is not found in certainty. It is found in the ability to hold space for multiple perspectives without the need to control, dismiss, or silence them.

Cognitive Dissonance: The Discomfort of Contradiction

When the mind encounters something that does not fit its existing framework, it resists. It labels, discredits, rationalizes—anything to avoid the discomfort of contradiction. This is the function of cognitive dissonance. It is the tension between what is known and what does not align.

Most avoid this tension. It feels threatening, as if an unstable foundation is being shaken. But what if the foundation itself was the illusion? What if the discomfort was not a sign to retreat, but an invitation to expand?

> *Fear does not arise from encountering new ideas—it arises from the mind's resistance to letting go of the old ones.*

Every moment of resistance is an opportunity. The discomfort that arises is not the problem; it is the gateway. It asks:

- Can I sit with this without needing to resolve it immediately?
- Can I question my own certainty without losing myself?
- Is my discomfort a sign that something here is worth exploring?

Growth does not happen in the absence of contradiction. It happens in the space where contradiction is observed without fear. When one learns to sit with this discomfort—to allow the mind to stretch rather than recoil—intellectual resilience is born.

The Social Cost of Dissent

To think freely is to risk rejection. To question widely accepted beliefs is to invite suspicion. The mind, conditioned to seek belonging, often chooses silence over truth.

There is a reason why so few step beyond the confines of social consensus. The price is high. When a person dares to see differently, to speak what is not meant to be spoken, they become an outsider. And for many, this is unbearable.

But what is the real cost of compliance? To remain in alignment with what is expected, even when it contradicts what is seen, is to betray something deeper within. It is to trade truth for comfort, awareness for approval.

And yet, the moment of liberation comes when one realizes: no one else holds the key to their freedom.

When the fear of dissent is no longer a barrier, when the need for approval dissolves, a new space opens—the space of unfiltered perception. Here, thought is no longer dictated by social pressure. Here, inquiry is no longer suppressed by fear.

The choice is simple, yet profound:

- Live confined by the approval of others, or step into the vastness of true awareness.
- Seek belonging at the cost of truth, or find truth at the risk of standing alone.

In the end, the greatest prison is not the judgment of others, but the fear of it. And the key has always been within.

Practical Strategies: Strengthening Independent Thought

The mind clings to what is familiar. It finds security in agreement, in the reinforcement of existing beliefs. But intellectual freedom is not found in comfort. It is forged in the willingness to step beyond what is known, to sit in the discomfort of contradiction, to allow the mind to stretch without retreating into defensiveness.

Independent thought is not about being contrarian for its own sake. It is about presence—awareness of thought without identification with it. The ability to examine an idea without the compulsion to defend or reject it. This is the space where true intelligence arises.

But how does one cultivate this? Not through theory alone, but through practice.

Growth does not happen in agreement. It happens in the space where certainty is undone, where the mind stretches beyond its own comfort.

Uncomfortable Ideas Challenge: Read the Opposition

Most people do not seek truth—they seek validation. They consume information that affirms their perspective, surrounding themselves with voices that echo their own. But growth happens not in agreement, but in challenge.

Choose a book, an article, or a podcast from a credible source that contradicts a belief you hold strongly. Not as an argument to dismantle, but as something to sit with. As you engage with the material, observe the mind:

- Do you feel tension rising?

- Are you already formulating counterarguments?

- Are you reading to understand, or simply to refute?

Now, shift the focus. Instead of looking for what is wrong, ask:

- What valid points does this perspective raise?

- Where might my own understanding be incomplete?

- How does this challenge or refine my viewpoint?

This is not about changing your beliefs. It is about loosening their grip. The tighter one holds onto certainty, the less they see. By consciously engaging with contradiction, the mind learns to open rather than close.

Outcome: Strengthen your capacity for critical engagement. Move beyond reaction into presence.

> *Read what unsettles you. Listen without reacting. Let go of the need to affirm what you already believe. In that space, the mind becomes free*

Cognitive Dissonance Reflection Journal

When an idea threatens what the mind has accepted as truth, discomfort arises. This is cognitive dissonance—the tension between what is believed and what is newly encountered. Most respond by dismissing or attacking the contradiction. But what if, instead, this discomfort became a doorway?

When confronted with an idea that unsettles you, pause. Instead of reacting, write down:

- What emotions did this trigger?

- Why might I feel defensive about this perspective?

- Is there any truth in this discomfort worth exploring?

The goal is not to force yourself to agree with everything, but to become aware of how the mind resists. This resistance is where intellectual growth is blocked. By observing it, you begin to dismantle its power.

Over time, this practice rewires the way you interact with challenging ideas. The mind learns that discomfort is not a threat but an opportunity. Instead of retreating into certainty, it expands.

Outcome: Recognize emotional responses that hinder intellectual growth. Learn to sit with contradiction rather than react to it.

Open Dialogue Practice: Host a Civil Debate

In an age where disagreement is seen as division, few engage in true dialogue. Conversations are reduced to debates, and debates to battles. But what if disagreement was not a conflict, but a practice in awareness?

Find someone who holds a different perspective from you. It could be political, philosophical, or personal. Organize a discussion—not to argue, but to listen.

Set ground rules:

- Listen without interrupting.

- Avoid personal attacks.

- Aim for understanding rather than winning.

During the conversation, notice where you feel the impulse to react. Where the body tenses. Where the mind begins crafting a rebuttal rather than absorbing what is being said.

Afterward, reflect:

- Did I truly listen, or was I waiting to respond?

- What was I defending? Was it truth, or was it my identity?

- How did engaging with this perspective influence my thinking?

True dialogue is not about persuasion. It is about presence. When you can hold space for ideas without the need to control them, intellectual freedom begins.

Outcome: Develop the ability to engage with differing viewpoints without attachment to being right.

The Practice of Intellectual Freedom

These exercises are not about adopting new beliefs, but about loosening identification with the ones you already hold. When the mind no longer reacts to contradiction with defensiveness, when it can sit with an opposing idea without losing itself, thought becomes fluid. No longer rigid. No longer confined.

And in that space, something deeper emerges—not just intelligence, but awareness.

Reflection and Action: Embracing Intellectual Challenge

The mind resists what it does not understand. It clings to familiarity, mistaking certainty for truth. But truth is not fixed. It moves, it expands, it reveals itself only to those willing to meet it without resistance.

> *Truth is not static. It moves, it reveals, it expands. To remain attached to a fixed perspective is to hold onto a past that no longer exists.*

To cultivate intellectual freedom is to become deeply aware of this resistance—not to fight it, but to observe it. The need to be right, the impulse to reject, the subtle tightening in the body when confronted with a different perspective—these are not signs of clarity but of conditioning.

The practice of independent thought is not an act of force, but of surrender. A willingness to let go of identification with beliefs, to see them as thoughts rather than as an extension of the self. It is in this space that transformation begins.

> *You are not your beliefs. You are the awareness that sees them, questions them, and, when necessary, releases them.*

The Freedom Beyond Certainty

Most people do not seek truth. They seek affirmation. They do not listen to understand, but to reinforce. And so, they remain trapped—not by external forces, but by their own unwillingness to let go.

But you are not most people.

If you can sit with discomfort, if you can observe your own resistance without becoming it, something profound happens. The need for certainty dissolves. The mind expands beyond what it thought it knew.

And in that expansion, freedom is not achieved. It is revealed.

"Freedom is the freedom to say that two plus two make four. If that is granted, all else follows."
— George Orwell

Outrage Addiction Insight

Why is it so difficult to engage with uncomfortable ideas?

Cognitive dissonance theory suggests that encountering conflicting beliefs triggers psychological discomfort, which the brain interprets as a threat.[1] This discomfort activates stress responses and discourages intellectual exploration. Studies have shown that confirmation bias—the tendency to seek information that aligns with pre-existing beliefs—stimulates the brain's reward system, reinforcing intellectual complacency.[2]

---

[1] *Festinger, 1957*
[2] *Nickerson, 1998*

The Road to Emotional Sovereignty

"He who controls others may be powerful, but he who has mastered himself is mightier still."

— *Lao Tzu*

Breaking Free from the Outrage Cycle

The Journey of Reclaiming Emotional Sovereignty

The world has conditioned you to remain in a state of reaction. It has trained you—quietly, persistently—to see offense as strength, to equate outrage with moral clarity. Each day, you are given new reasons to react, new enemies to condemn, new injustices to rage against. And yet, beneath it all, there is exhaustion.

You have felt it. The heaviness of being on guard. The weariness of constantly justifying your emotions, proving your righteousness, defending yourself against those who do not see the world as you do. The endless cycle of reaction consumes more than your energy; it consumes your peace.

But awareness changes everything. The moment you see the pattern, the moment you step back and observe it without immediately engaging, the grip of outrage begins to loosen. You realize that you are not required to play this game. That participation is not a duty—it is a choice. And that choice has always been yours.

This is what it means to reclaim emotional sovereignty. It is not about disengaging from the world, nor about ignoring injustice. It is about responding from clarity rather than compulsion. It is about recognizing the difference between presence and reactivity, between true action and conditioned reaction.

The world may still present you with reasons to be outraged. But it no longer decides for you.

The Hidden Costs of Outrage Addiction

Outrage is not free. It may feel momentarily empowering, like a surge of certainty, a righteous fire burning in the mind. But this fire consumes more than it illuminates.

The personal cost is subtle at first. A loss of inner peace. A sense of restlessness, of always needing to check, to respond, to correct. Relationships become strained, as dialogue gives way to defensiveness, as listening is replaced with the impulse to refute. Conversations become battles. Human beings become caricatures of right and wrong, ally or enemy.

The psychological toll is heavier still. A mind conditioned to outrage is never at rest. It finds offense even in silence. It searches for conflict where none exists, because conflict has become familiar, even comfortable. The nervous system remains in a constant state of stress, reacting as though each disagreement is a threat, each differing opinion an attack.

And then, there is the societal cost. A culture addicted to outrage cannot grow. It cannot think freely, because it is too afraid of saying the wrong thing. It cannot progress, because it has mistaken performative anger for meaningful action. In a world where nuance is lost, dialogue is impossible. And where dialogue is impossible, division thrives.

None of this is accidental. Outrage is a product, sold to you daily. It is reinforced by algorithms, by media cycles, by institutions that profit from keeping you engaged, angry, and distracted. But you do not have to buy into it.

You are not obligated to carry the weight of every headline, every controversy, every passing storm of collective anger. You are allowed to step back. To breathe. To choose where your energy goes.

This is not weakness. It is power.

The Power of Emotional Autonomy

There is a space between stimulus and response. A moment of stillness in which all things are possible. Most people never access it. They react without pause, without awareness, trapped in the momentum of their emotions. But you are beginning to see that there is another way.

Emotional autonomy is the realization that no one can dictate your inner state but you. It is the understanding that anger, while sometimes justified, does not have to consume you. That disagreement does not have to mean conflict. That silence does not have to mean surrender.

When you are no longer controlled by external noise, clarity arises. You see the world not through the lens of reaction, but through the lens of presence. You can respond—calmly, intentionally—without being pulled into the chaos around you.

This is true empowerment. Not the fleeting power of outrage, which vanishes the moment it is expressed, but the quiet, unshakable power of presence.

The world will continue as it always has. It will tempt you with new reasons to be outraged. It will insist that you must react. But you will know the truth:

You are free.

Key Lessons from The Outrage Paradox

Recognizing Outrage as a Psychological Addiction

Outrage does not arise in isolation. It is part of a deeply conditioned pattern, reinforced by external stimuli and internal reward mechanisms. Each moment of anger, each impulse to react, carries with it a surge of energy—a feeling of certainty, of righteousness. This momentary high is not unlike any other addiction. It feels good. It feels necessary. And so, it continues.

The mind seeks repetition. It learns what brings validation, what elicits a response, what makes it feel alive, even if that aliveness is rooted in conflict. The cycle repeats itself—an external provocation, an emotional response, a sense of temporary satisfaction, followed by the need for more.

This is how outrage becomes an unconscious habit. It becomes embedded in the nervous system, a conditioned response that feels automatic. The body tenses before the mind even knows why. The pulse quickens, the breath shortens, and before awareness has a chance to intervene, the reaction is set in motion.

But there is another way. To break free from this cycle, one must first recognize it—not intellectually, but through direct awareness. Observe the moment outrage arises. Feel the physical sensation of it. Notice the impulse to act, to correct, to defend. Then, without suppressing it, simply allow it to be. Do not follow it. Do not justify it. Just see it.

Something remarkable happens in that space of awareness. The pattern weakens. The automatic response loses its hold. And in its place, a choice emerges.

This is the beginning of freedom.

The Personal and Societal Costs of Outrage Culture

What does outrage take from you?

At first, it seems to offer power. A sense of being right, of standing for something, of belonging to a collective movement. But over time, the cost becomes apparent.

Outrage erodes peace. It keeps the mind in a state of tension, the body in a state of stress. It fosters conflict where connection is needed, turns dialogue into opposition, relationships into battlegrounds.

It diminishes intellectual freedom. When outrage governs thought, curiosity is replaced with certainty. There is no space to ask, "Could I be wrong?" or "Is there another way to see this?" Instead, the mind becomes rigid, clinging to its perspective as though it were an identity.

And on a larger scale, this conditioning shapes society itself. A culture addicted to outrage is a culture divided. It becomes incapable of nuance, unable to hold space for differences. It fosters fear—fear of speaking, fear of being misunderstood, fear of existing outside the approved narrative. And in this fear, authentic dialogue disappears.

A divided world is easier to control. A world where people see enemies instead of fellow human beings, where reaction replaces reflection, is a world that remains stagnant. The mechanisms that profit from outrage—whether through media, politics, or social validation—depend on this division.

But this division is not inevitable. Awareness makes it optional.

The moment you step outside the cycle, you see it for what it is. And in seeing, you reclaim your power.

The Power of Emotional Resilience, Empathy, and Intellectual Freedom

True power does not come from reacting. It comes from choosing how, and whether, to engage.

Emotional resilience is the ability to remain unmoved by the tides of external provocation. It does not mean indifference, nor does it mean suppression. It means presence. The ability to witness emotions arise without being overtaken by them. The ability to engage with the world without losing yourself in it.

This resilience allows space for genuine empathy. Not the performative kind that seeks validation, but the quiet, steady kind that listens without agenda. When you are no longer caught in your own emotional storms, you can be fully present with another. You can hear them, not as an opponent, but as another human being—complex, struggling, just as you are.

And with this presence comes intellectual freedom. The capacity to think independently, to hold space for uncertainty, to engage with ideas that challenge your own without defensiveness. A mind no longer controlled by outrage becomes a mind that can truly explore, truly grow.

This is what it means to be free. Not free from the world, but free within it. Free to engage without attachment, to care without being consumed, to think without fear.

The world will continue to call you into reaction. But now, you will see the choice.

And in that choice, you will find your sovereignty.

Long-Term Action Plan: Sustaining Emotional Sovereignty

Emotional sovereignty is not a one-time realization. It is a practice, a way of being that must be nurtured and sustained. The world will continue to present opportunities to fall back into reaction—to be pulled into cycles of outrage, division, and unconscious emotional responses. But with awareness, these same moments become invitations to deepen your presence, to strengthen your inner stillness, to live with intention rather than reactivity.

The following practices serve as a guide—a way to continue cultivating resilience, mindfulness, and clarity in a world that thrives on distraction and emotional turbulence.

Weekly Emotional Awareness Check-Ins

Awareness is not passive. It is an active engagement with the present moment, a willingness to observe without judgment. To sustain emotional sovereignty, reflection must become part of your practice—a regular opportunity to notice patterns, identify triggers, and refine your responses.

Each week, set aside time to ask yourself:

– What triggered me this week? Was there a particular conversation, event, or piece of media that caused a strong reaction?

– How did I respond emotionally? Did I react impulsively, or was I able to pause and observe my emotions?

– What could I do differently next time? If the same situation arose again, how might I engage with more awareness and less reactivity?

Write these reflections down. Not as a way to dwell on the past, but to bring clarity to the present. Patterns emerge when they are seen. And in seeing them, their hold on you begins to weaken.

Each moment of unconscious reaction is not a failure. It is simply another opportunity to wake up.

Regular Mindfulness and Cognitive Reframing Practice

Stillness is a practice. Like any muscle, it strengthens with use. A daily mindfulness routine serves as an anchor—a way to cultivate a state of presence that is not easily shaken by external forces.

Commit to a simple practice:

1. Begin each morning with stillness. Before reaching for a phone, before engaging with the world, take a moment to breathe. Sit in silence. Observe the mind. Notice any lingering tension. Recognize that you are not your thoughts— you are the awareness that observes them.

2. Reframe triggers as neutral stimuli. Throughout the day, when faced with a potential outrage trigger, practice reframing. Instead of seeing an event as inherently offensive or threatening, pause and ask:

– "What if this is just information?"

– "What if my reaction is learned rather than necessary?"

– "Can I observe without engaging emotionally?"

3. End the day with release. Before sleeping, reflect on any moments of tension or emotional charge. Consciously let them go. Visualize them dissolving. The past exists only in the mind—there is no need to carry it into tomorrow.

These small, daily practices create profound shifts over time. The less reactive the mind becomes, the more space there is for peace.

Continued Avoidance of Outrage-Driven Media

Not all information is nourishment. Some media exists not to inform, but to provoke. To sustain emotional sovereignty, it is essential to become intentional about what you consume.

1. Limit exposure to outrage-inducing content. This does not mean disengaging from the world, but rather choosing how and when to engage. Notice which sources fuel anger, division, and emotional turbulence. If something consistently pulls you into reaction, step away.

2. Replace reactive consumption with mindful engagement. Instead of mindlessly scrolling through social media or news designed to elicit outrage, choose sources that encourage depth, nuance, and understanding. Ask yourself:

    – "Does this content expand my awareness or reinforce my emotions?"

    – "Am I engaging out of curiosity, or am I seeking validation for my outrage?"

    – "What would happen if I stepped away from this entirely?"

3. Create space for silence. In a world that constantly demands attention, stillness is a radical act. Set boundaries around media consumption. Create moments in your day that are free from external noise. Listen to the quiet. This is where true clarity arises.

The Practice of Sovereignty

Emotional sovereignty is not about withdrawal. It is not about disengaging from important issues or avoiding difficult conversations. It is about choosing how to engage—with clarity rather than compulsion, with presence rather than reaction.

Each choice to pause, to reflect, to disengage from the cycle of outrage is a step toward freedom.

And the more you choose this freedom, the more natural it becomes.

"No one can make you feel inferior without your consent."
                                   — Eleanor Roosevelt

Final Reflection: Embracing Emotional Sovereignty

The world will not change. It will continue to move in cycles of conflict, reaction, and distraction. The outrage machine will not stop producing new reasons to be offended, new enemies to fight, new battles to win. But you do not have to participate.

True freedom does not come from silencing others, nor from proving oneself right. It does not come from winning arguments, accumulating allies, or mastering the language of moral superiority. It comes from stepping outside the cycle entirely. From realizing that your peace does not depend on what the world is doing, but on how you choose to engage with it.

The power has always been yours.

The Freedom of Choosing Your Reaction

What does it mean to be free? Most people think freedom is external—the ability to speak, to act, to assert one's beliefs without restriction. But the deeper freedom is internal. It is the freedom to remain unmoved by external forces. The freedom to feel without being consumed. The freedom to observe without being controlled.

This is emotional sovereignty. It is the moment you realize that nothing—no comment, no opinion, no event—has the power to dictate your emotional state unless you allow it.

Outrage culture thrives on reaction. It requires your participation. It demands that you take a side, that you feel the anger, that you reinforce the narrative. But you can simply step back. You can breathe. You can watch as the mind wants to engage, as it feels the pull of reaction, and in that moment, you can choose.

Not from suppression. Not from avoidance. But from presence.

When you are no longer a servant to reaction, you are free.

Reclaiming Peace in a Hyper-Reactive World

The world is loud. It rewards the loud. But the loud are not at peace.

Reactionary living creates tension. The constant scanning for offense, the need to defend, the weight of being on high alert—it is exhausting. And yet, this is how so many live, believing they are engaged, believing they are fighting for something, when in reality, they are simply trapped in a state of perpetual distress.

Peace is not apathy. It is not indifference. It is not a refusal to act. It is the ability to act without being driven by compulsion. It is engagement without attachment. It is the clarity to see when speaking up serves a purpose and when silence is the wiser path.

A reactive world does not need more voices shouting into the void. It needs more people rooted in stillness. It needs those who can hold space without being drawn into the storm.

To reclaim peace is not to withdraw. It is to be present, to engage with life from a place of deep awareness rather than emotional impulse.

It is to recognize that there is nothing to prove. That there is nothing to defend. That the self you are so eager to protect is merely a collection of thoughts—temporary, shifting, and ultimately insignificant.

And when that truth settles in, what is left?

Silence.

Not emptiness, but space.

And in that space, you are finally free.

The Call to Live Intentionally

This is not a call to disengage from the world, but to engage with greater awareness. To move through life not as a pawn of external forces, but as a witness, an observer, a conscious participant.

Every moment presents a choice. To react or to pause. To fuel the fire or to step away. To be consumed by the collective hysteria or to remain steady in the face of it.

Most will continue as they always have. They will seek out offense, they will identify with their emotions, they will defend their anger as though it is their identity. But you have another path.

Not an easy path. Not a path that will bring you validation or applause. But a path of deep, unshakable peace.

Live with intention. Move with awareness. Speak only when words serve truth, and be silent when they do not.

And when the world pulls at you, when it demands a reaction, when it insists that you must be outraged, that you must be offended, that you must participate in the endless cycle of conflict—

Pause.

Breathe.

Step back.

And remember: You are already free.

"The greatest discovery of any generation is that a human being can alter his life by altering his attitude." — William James

Bibliography

Abbot, D. (2021). *Letter to the public on free inquiry in science.* https://www.dorianabbot.com

Abidin, C. (2018). *Internet celebrity: Understanding fame online.* Emerald Publishing.

Applebaum, A. (2012). *Iron curtain: The crushing of Eastern Europe, 1944–1956.* Doubleday.

Atlantic, The. (2020, June 3). *Instagram's Black Square trend and the problem with performative activism.* https://www.theatlantic.com/

Bandura, A. (1997). *Self-efficacy: The exercise of control.* W. H. Freeman.

Banet-Weiser, S. (2018). *Empowered: Popular feminism and popular misogyny.* Duke University Press.

Bail, C. A., Argyle, L. P., Brown, T. W., Bumpus, J. P., Chen, H., Hunzaker, M. B. F., ... & Volfovsky, A. (2018). Exposure to opposing views on social media can increase political polarization. *Proceedings of the National Academy of Sciences, 115*(37), 9216–9221. https://doi.org/10.1073/pnas.1804840115

Baron, J. (2008). *Thinking and deciding* (4th ed.). Cambridge University Press.

Bartholomew, R. E. (2017). *A colorblind America: How the left lost its mind over race.* Prometheus Books.

Batson, C. D. (2011). *Altruism in humans.* Oxford University Press.

Baumeister, R. F., & Leary, M. R. (1995). The need to belong: Desire for interpersonal attachments as a fundamental human motivation. *Psychological Bulletin, 117*(3), 497–529. https://doi.org/10.1037/0033-2909.117.3.497

Belenky, M. F., Clinchy, B. M., Goldberger, N. R., & Tarule, J. M. (1986). *Women's ways of knowing: The development of self, voice, and mind.* Basic Books.

Bloom, P. (2016). *Against empathy: The case for rational compassion.* HarperCollins.

Baumeister, R. F., & Tierney, J. (2011). *Willpower: Rediscovering the greatest human strength*. Penguin Press.

BBC News. (2017, April 5). *Pepsi pulls controversial Kendall Jenner advert*. https://www.bbc.com/news

BBC News. (2020, June 18). *How social media outrage led to emotional exhaustion during BLM protests*. https://www.bbc.com/

BBC News. (2021, June 15). *Chrissy Teigen apologizes over online bullying claims*. https://www.bbc.com/news/

BBC News. (2021, June 22). *Billie Eilish apologizes after backlash over old video*. https://www.bbc.com/

BBC News. (2022, November 24). *Balenciaga controversy: How the fashion house sparked global backlash*. https://www.bbc.com/

Berger, J., & Milkman, K. L. (2012). What makes online content viral? *Journal of Marketing Research, 49*(2), 192–205. https://doi.org/10.1509/jmr.10.0353

Block, J., & Kremen, A. M. (1996). IQ and ego-resiliency: Conceptual and empirical connections and separateness. *Journal of Personality and Social Psychology, 70*(2), 349–361. https://doi.org/10.1037/0022-3514.70.2.349

Bonanno, G. A. (2004). Loss, trauma, and human resilience: Have we underestimated the human capacity to thrive after extremely aversive events? *American Psychologist, 59*(1), 20–28. https://doi.org/10.1037/0003-066X.59.1.20

Boyd, D. M., Vosoughi, S., & Roy, D. (2020). The emotional impact of digital outrage: Psychological and physiological consequences of online conflict. *Journal of Experimental Psychology, 149*(3), 458–472. https://doi.org/10.1037/xge0000661

Brady, W. J., Wills, J. A., Jost, J. T., Tucker, J. A., & Van Bavel, J. J. (2021). Emotion shapes the diffusion of moralized content in social networks. *Proceedings of the National Academy of Sciences, 118*(28), e2016184118. https://doi.org/10.1073/pnas.2016184118

Brown, R. (2016). *Honor: A history*. Encounter Books.

Brownstone Institute. (2021). *Public health and the limits of censorship*. https://brownstone.org

Bloom, P. (2017). *Against empathy: The case for rational compassion*. HarperCollins.

Brady, W. J., Wills, J. A., Jost, J. T., Tucker, J. A., & Van Bavel, J. J. (2017). Emotion shapes the diffusion of moralized content in social networks. *Proceedings of the National Academy of Sciences, 114*(28), 7313–7318. https://doi.org/10.1073/pnas.1618923114

Business Insider. (2020, June 2). *H&M accused of performative activism after BLM post*. https://www.businessinsider.com/

Cameron, C. D., & Payne, B. K. (2011). Escaping affect: How motivated emotion regulation creates insensitivity to mass suffering. *Journal of Personality and Social Psychology, 100*(1), 1–15. https://doi.org/10.1037/a0021643

Cato Institute. (2020). *The state of free speech and tolerance in America.* https://www.cato.org

Chater, N. (2018). *The mind is flat: The remarkable shallowness of the improvising brain.* Yale University Press.

Chatterjee, P., & Finger, M. (2020). *The earth brokers: Power, politics, and world development* (2nd ed.). Routledge.

Chicago Tribune. (2019, March 8). *Jussie Smollett indicted on 16 counts related to alleged attack.* https://www.chicagotribune.com/

Chomsky, N., & Herman, E. S. (1988). *Manufacturing consent: The political economy of the mass media.* Pantheon Books.

Chou, H. T. G., & Edge, N. (2012). "They are happier and having better lives than I am": The impact of using Facebook on perceptions of others' lives. *Cyberpsychology, Behavior, and Social Networking, 15*(2), 117–121. https://doi.org/10.1089/cyber.2011.0324

Chouinard, Y. (2022). *Let my people go surfing: The education of a reluctant businessman.* Penguin.

Christakis, N. (2020). *Blueprint: The evolutionary origins of a good society.* Little, Brown Spark.

CNN Business. (2018, September 9). *Nike sales surge after Colin Kaepernick ad campaign.* https://www.cnn.com/business

Crockett, M. J. (2017). Moral outrage in the digital age. *Nature Human Behaviour, 1*(11), 769–771. https://doi.org/10.1038/s41562-017-0213-3

Croucher, M. (2023, April 18). How a beer ad sparked a culture war—and lost millions. *The Guardian.* https://www.theguardian.com

Davis, D. (1998). *Klan-destine relationships: A Black man's odyssey in the Ku Klux Klan.* New Horizon Press.

Decety, J., & Lamm, C. (2006). Human empathy through the lens of social neuroscience. *The Scientific World Journal, 6*, 1146–1163. https://doi.org/10.1100/tsw.2006.221

Del Vicario, M., Bessi, A., Zollo, F., Petroni, F., Scala, A., Caldarelli, G., Stanley, H. E., & Quattrociocchi, W. (2016). The spreading of misinformation online. *Proceedings of the National Academy of Sciences, 113*(3), 554–559. https://doi.org/10.1073/pnas.1517441113

Doherty, C., & Kiley, J. (2020). In a politically polarized era, fewer Americans hold a mix of conservative and liberal views. *Pew Research Center.* https://www.pewresearch.org/

Dweck, C. S. (2006). *Mindset: The new psychology of success.* Random House.

Edelman Trust Barometer. (2022). *Public trust in media and institutions report.* https://www.edelman.com

Eisenberger, N. I., Lieberman, M. D., & Williams, K. D. (2003). Does rejection hurt? An fMRI study of social exclusion. *Science, 302*(5643), 290–292. https://doi.org/10.1126/science.1089134

Festinger, L. (1957). *A theory of cognitive dissonance.* Stanford University Press.

Figley, C. R. (1995). *Compassion fatigue: Coping with secondary traumatic stress disorder in those who treat the traumatized.* Brunner-Routledge.

Figley, C. R. (2002). Compassion fatigue: Psychotherapists' chronic lack of self-care. *Journal of Clinical Psychology, 58*(11), 1433–1441. https://doi.org/10.1002/jclp.10090

Finkel, E. J., Bail, C. A., Cikara, M., Ditto, P. H., Iyengar, S., Klar, S., & Van Bavel, J. J. (2020). Political sectarianism in America. *Science, 370*(6516), 533–536. https://doi.org/10.1126/science.abe1715

Fredrickson, B. L. (2001). The role of positive emotions in positive psychology: The broaden-and-build theory of positive emotions. *American Psychologist, 56*(3), 218–226. https://doi.org/10.1037/0003-066X.56.3.218

Frontline. (2016). *Accidental courtesy: Daryl Davis, race & America* [Documentary]. PBS. https://www.pbs.org/show/frontline/

Fuchs, C. (2022). *Digital capitalism: Media, communication and society.* Routledge.

Furedi, F. (2016). *What's happened to the university? A sociological exploration of its infantilisation.* Routledge.

Gallup. (2021). *Americans' trust in media edges down to record low.* Gallup Polls. https://news.gallup.com/

Gilbert, P. (2010). *The compassionate mind: A new approach to life's challenges.* New Harbinger.

Ginsburg, R. B. (2016). *My own words.* Simon & Schuster.

Giridharadas, A. (2018). *Winners take all: The elite charade of changing the world.* Knopf.

Goetz, J. L., Keltner, D., & Simon-Thomas, E. (2010). Compassion: An evolutionary analysis and empirical review. *Psychological Bulletin, 136*(3), 351–374. https://doi.org/10.1037/a0018807

Gross, J. J. (2002). Emotion regulation: Affective, cognitive, and social consequences. *Psychophysiology, 39*(3), 281–291. https://doi.org/10.1017/S0048577201393198

Gross, J. J., & John, O. P. (2003). Individual differences in two emotion regulation processes: Implications for affect, relationships, and well-being. *Journal of Personality and Social Psychology, 85*(2), 348–362. https://doi.org/10.1037/0022-3514.85.2.348

Grynbaum, M. M., & Tracy, M. (2020, June 7). James Bennet resigns as *New York Times* editorial page editor. *The New York Times.* https://www.nytimes.com

Habermas, J. (1989). *The structural transformation of the public sphere: An inquiry into a category of bourgeois society* (T. Burger & F. Lawrence, Trans.). MIT Press. (Original work published 1962)

Haidt, J. (2012). *The righteous mind: Why good people are divided by politics and religion.* Pantheon Books.

Haidt, J., & Lukianoff, G. (2018). *The coddling of the American mind: How good intentions and bad ideas are setting up a generation for failure.* Penguin Press.

Hanania, R. (2021). The incentive structures of modern media: How outrage drives profits. *Journal of Political Psychology, 14*(2), 178–194. https://doi.org/10.1037/1089-2680.14.2.178

Harper's Magazine. (2020, July). A letter on justice and open debate. *Harper's Magazine.* https://harpers.org

Herman, E. S., & Chomsky, N. (2002). *Propaganda model revisited: The economics of media bias.* Cambridge University Press.

Hindman, M. (2018). *The internet trap: How the digital economy builds monopolies and undermines democracy.* Princeton University Press.

Iyengar, S., & Westwood, S. J. (2015). Fear and loathing across party lines: New evidence on group polarization. *American Journal of Political Science, 59*(3), 690–707. https://doi.org/10.1111/ajps.12152

JAMA Network. (2021). *Physician burnout and mental health during the COVID-19 pandemic.* https://jamanetwork.com/

Jordan, J., Sommers, R., Bloom, P., & Rand, D. G. (2016). Why do we hate hypocrites? Evidence for a theory of false signaling. *Psychological Science, 27*(10), 1448–1456. https://doi.org/10.1177/0956797616662104

Kahneman, D. (2011). *Thinking, fast and slow.* Farrar, Straus and Giroux.

Kashdan, T. B., & Rottenberg, J. (2010). Psychological flexibility as a fundamental aspect of health. *Clinical Psychology Review, 30*(7), 865–878. https://doi.org/10.1016/j.cpr.2010.03.001

Klimecki, O. M., Ricard, M., & Singer, T. (2013). Empathy versus compassion: Distinct neural responses to suffering. *Social Cognitive and Affective Neuroscience, 9*(6), 873–879. https://doi.org/10.1093/scan/nst239

Knight Foundation. (2021). *Free expression on campus report.* https://knightfoundation.org

Konrath, S., O'Brien, E. H., & Hsing, C. (2011). Changes in dispositional empathy in American college students over time: A meta-analysis. *Personality and Social Psychology Review, 15*(2), 180–198. https://doi.org/10.1177/1088868310377395

Kunda, Z. (1990). The case for motivated reasoning. *Psychological Bulletin, 108*(3), 480–498. https://doi.org/10.1037/0033-2909.108.3.480

Lakoff, G. (2004). *Don't think of an elephant!: Know your values and frame the debate.* Chelsea Green Publishing.

Lamm, C., Batson, C. D., & Decety, J. (2007). The neural substrate of human empathy: Effects of perspective-taking and cognitive appraisal. *Journal of Cognitive Neuroscience, 19*(1), 42–58. https://doi.org/10.1162/jocn.2007.19.1.42

Lanier, J. (2018). *Ten arguments for deleting your social media accounts right now.* Henry Holt and Co.

Lasch, C. (1979). *The culture of narcissism: American life in an age of diminishing expectations.* W. W. Norton & Company.

Leary, M. R., & Kowalski, R. M. (1990). Impression management: A literature review and two-component model. *Psychological Bulletin, 107*(1), 34–47. https://doi.org/10.1037/0033-2909.107.1.34

LeDoux, J. E. (2000). Emotion circuits in the brain. *Annual Review of Neuroscience, 23*(1), 155–184. https://doi.org/10.1146/annurev.neuro.23.1.155

Loury, G. C. (2021). *The anatomy of racial inequality* (2nd ed.). Harvard University Press.

Loury, G. C. (2021). *Race, injustice, and the limits of progressive thought.* Free Press.

Lukianoff, G., & Haidt, J. (2018). *The coddling of the American mind: How good intentions and bad ideas are setting up a generation for failure.* Penguin Press.

Maier, S. F., & Seligman, M. E. (2016). Learned helplessness at fifty: Insights from neuroscience. *Psychological Review, 123*(4), 349–367. https://doi.org/10.1037/rev0000033

McBride, K. (2020). The rush to judgment: How media mishandled the Covington Catholic story. *Poynter Institute.* https://www.poynter.org

McCann, I. L., & Pearlman, L. A. (1990). Vicarious traumatization: A framework for understanding the psychological effects of working with victims. *Journal of Traumatic Stress, 3*(1), 131–149. https://doi.org/10.1007/BF00975140

McChesney, R. W. (2015). *Rich media, poor democracy: Communication politics in dubious times.* The New Press.

McEwen, B. S. (2007). Physiology and neurobiology of stress and adaptation: Central role of the brain. *Physiological Reviews, 87*(3), 873–904. https://doi.org/10.1152/physrev.00041.2006

McLuhan, M. (1964). *Understanding media: The extensions of man.* McGraw-Hill.

McNair, B. (2017). *An introduction to political communication* (6th ed.). Routledge.

Medvedev, Z. (1969). *The rise and fall of T.D. Lysenko.* Columbia University Press.

Mercier, H., & Sperber, D. (2017). *The enigma of reason.* Harvard University Press.

Meshi, D., Tamir, D. I., & Heekeren, H. R. (2015). The emerging neuroscience of social media. *Trends in Cognitive Sciences, 19*(12), 771–782. https://doi.org/10.1016/j.tics.2015.09.004

Mihaylov, N., & Perkins, D. D. (2015). Political engagement and emotional burnout in digital activism. *Journal of Applied Social Psychology, 45*(9), 488–499. https://doi.org/10.1111/jasp.12308

Mounk, Y. (2020, July 3). The canceling of David Shor. *The Atlantic.* https://www.theatlantic.com

Munger, K. (2020). The rise of partisan media and the decline of objective journalism. *Social Media & Society, 6*(1), 1–13. https://doi.org/10.1177/2056305120915176

Neff, K. (2011). *Self-compassion: The proven power of being kind to yourself.* HarperCollins.

Neveu, J. P. (2007). Jailed by the job: Burnout in social service workers. *Journal of Applied Psychology, 92*(5), 1367–1377. https://doi.org/10.1037/0021-9010.92.5.1367

Nichols, T. (2017). *The death of expertise: The campaign against established knowledge and why it matters.* Oxford University Press.

Nickerson, R. S. (1998). Confirmation bias: A ubiquitous phenomenon in many guises. *Review of General Psychology, 2*(2), 175–220. https://doi.org/10.1037/1089-2680.2.2.175

Noelle-Neumann, E. (1993). *The spiral of silence: Public opinion—Our social skin* (2nd ed.). University of Chicago Press.

Orben, A., Przybylski, A. K., Blakemore, S. J., & Hagan, C. C. (2020). The association between social media use and mental health: A meta-analysis of time spent online and psychological well-being. *Journal of the American Academy of Child & Adolescent Psychiatry, 59*(6), 686–697. https://doi.org/10.1016/j.jaac.2019.12.002

Pennycook, G., & Rand, D. G. (2019). The psychology of fake news. *Trends in Cognitive Sciences, 23*(5), 372–390. https://doi.org/10.1016/j.tics.2019.01.006

Pariser, E. (2011). *The filter bubble: What the internet is hiding from you.* Penguin Press.

Pennycook, G., & Rand, D. G. (2019). The psychology of fake news. *Trends in Cognitive Sciences, 23*(5), 372–390. https://doi.org/10.1016/j.tics.2019.01.006

Peterson, C. (2006). *A primer in positive psychology.* Oxford University Press.

Petersen, M. B., Osmundsen, M., & Arceneaux, K. (2018). A "need for chaos" and the sharing of hostile political rumors in advanced democracies. *Psychological Science, 29*(11), 1711–1720. https://doi.org/10.1177/0956797618796480

Pew Research Center. (2021). *Political polarization and social cohesion in the 21st century.* https://www.pewresearch.org

Pew Research Center. (2021, October 13). *How outrage exhaustion is shaping political engagement in America.* https://www.pewresearch.org/

Pinker, S. (2011). *The better angels of our nature: Why violence has declined.* Penguin.

Pinker, S. (2018). *The sense of style: The thinking person's guide to writing in the 21st century.* Penguin Books.

Pinker, S. (2020). *Rationality: What It Is, Why It Seems Scarce, and Why It Matters.*

Potenza, M. N., Hong, K. A., & Lacadie, C. M. (2019). Neural correlates of stress-induced and cue-induced craving: Influences of gender and sex hormones. *The Journal of Neuroscience, 39*(1), 195–211. https://doi.org/10.1523/JNEUROSCI.2320-18.2018

Rauch, J. (2021). *The constitution of knowledge: A defense of truth.* Brookings Institution Press..

Reilly, K. (2021, February 26). Coca-Cola's diversity training controversy. *TIME.* https://time.com

Rose, M. (2012). The manipulation of visual media in modern journalism. *Columbia Journalism Review.* https://www.cjr.org

Rothschild, Z. K., & Keefer, L. A. (2017). A cleansing fire: Moral outrage alleviates guilt and buffers threats to one's moral identity. *Motivation and Emotion, 41*(2), 209–229. https://doi.org/10.1007/s11031-017-9601-6

Sapolsky, R. M. (2004). *Why zebras don't get ulcers* (3rd ed.). Holt Paperbacks.

Rowling, J. K. (2021, July 14). Statement on free speech and women's rights. https://www.jkrowling.com

Scalia, A., & Ginsburg, R. B. (2015, October 29). *Opera and the Court: An unlikely friendship* [Interview]. National Press Club. https://www.press.org/

Schultz, W. (2016). Dopamine reward prediction error coding. *Dialogues in Clinical Neuroscience, 18*(1), 23–32. https://doi.org/10.31887/DCNS.2016.18.1/wschultz

Schwartz, A. (2019, March 21). The Southern Poverty Law Center's list of hate groups is long. Maybe too long. *The Atlantic.* https://www.theatlantic.com

Sedikides, C., & Gregg, A. P. (2008). Self-enhancement: Food for thought. *Perspectives on Psychological Science, 3*(2), 102–116. https://doi.org/10.1111/j.1745-6916.2008.00068.x

Seligman, M. E. P. (2011). *Flourish: A visionary new understanding of happiness and well-being.* Free Press.

Sexton, J. (2021). The Jussie Smollett trial: A media reckoning. *New York Post.* https://nypost.com

Shaw, J. (2021). Smith College and the push for ideological compliance in the workplace: Resignation letter and public statement. *Bari Weiss Substack*. https://www.thefp.com

Shaw, J. (2021, March 4). Why I resigned from Smith College: I was publicly shamed for questioning a culture of race-based assumptions. *Common Sense with Bari Weiss*. https://www.thefp.com/

Slovic, P. (2007). "If I look at the mass, I will never act": Psychic numbing and genocide. *Judgment and Decision Making, 2*(2), 79–95. https://journal.sjdm.org/jdm7303.pdf

Soroka, S., Fournier, P., & Nir, L. (2019). Cross-national evidence of a negativity bias in psychophysiological reactions to news. *Proceedings of the National Academy of Sciences, 116*(38), 18888–18892. https://doi.org/10.1073/pnas.1908369116

Sowell, T. (1987). *A conflict of visions: Ideological origins of political struggles.* William Morrow.

Stock, K. (2021). *Material girls: Why reality matters for feminism.* Fleet.

Sunstein, C. R. (2003). *Why societies need dissent.* Harvard University Press.

Sunstein, C. R. (2009). *Going to extremes: How like minds unite and divide.* Oxford University Press.

Sunstein, C. R. (2009). *Republic.com 2.0.* Princeton University Press.

Suler, J. (2004). The online disinhibition effect. *CyberPsychology & Behavior, 7*(3), 321–326. https://doi.org/10.1089/1094931041291295

The Guardian. (2019, December 12). *Greta Thunberg on climate anxiety and activism burnout.* https://www.theguardian.com/

The Guardian. (2020, June 10). *JK Rowling defends right to speak on transgender issues despite criticism.* https://www.theguardian.com/

The Washington Post. (2022, March 3). *Ukraine crisis: Social media users face backlash for 'not caring enough'.* https://www.washingtonpost.com/

Tufekci, Z. (2015). Algorithmic filtering and ideological amplification: How social media shapes public opinion. *The Atlantic.* https://www.theatlantic.com

Tufekci, Z. (2015). Algorithmic harms beyond Facebook and Google: Emergent challenges of computational agency. *Colorado Technology Law Journal, 13*(1), 203–218. https://ctlj.colorado.edu/?p=1310

Tufekci, Z. (2015). Engineering the public: Big data, surveillance, and computational politics. *Journal of Information Technology & Politics, 13*(1), 1–24. https://doi.org/10.1080/19331681.2015.1130651

Tufekci, Z. (2015). *Twitter and tear gas: The power and fragility of networked protest.* Yale University Press.

Turel, O., He, Q., Xue, G., Xiao, L., & Bechara, A. (2014). Examination of neural systems sub-serving Facebook "addiction." *Psychological Reports: Disability and Trauma, 115*(3), 675–695. https://doi.org/10.2466/18.PR0.115c31z8

Twenge, J. M., Spitzberg, B. H., & Campbell, W. K. (2018). Less in-person social interaction with peers among U.S. adolescents in the 21st century and links to loneliness. *Journal of Social and Personal Relationships, 35*(10), 1344–1367. https://doi.org/10.1177/0265407517699784

van der Kolk, B. (2014). *The body keeps the score: Brain, mind, and body in the healing of trauma.* Viking.

Variety. (2020, July 30). *Inside Ellen DeGeneres' toxic workplace scandal.* https://variety.com/

Volkow, N. D., Fowler, J. S., & Wang, G. J. (2011). The addicted human brain viewed in the light of imaging studies: Brain circuits and treatment strategies. *Neuropharmacology, 56*(Suppl 1), 3–8. https://doi.org/10.1016/j.neuropharm.2010.07.019

Vosoughi, S., Roy, D., & Aral, S. (2018). The spread of true and false news online. *Science, 359*(6380), 1146–1151. https://doi.org/10.1126/science.aap9559

Waytz, A., Dungan, J., & Young, L. (2015). The whistleblower's dilemma and the fairness–loyalty tradeoff. *Journal of Experimental Social Psychology, 59*, 96–104. https://doi.org/10.1016/j.jesp.2015.03.003

Weinstein, B. (2017). Resignation letter to Evergreen State College. https://bretweinstein.net

Weinstein, B., & Heying, H. A. (2021). *A hunter-gatherer's guide to the 21st century: Evolution and the challenges of modern life.* Portfolio.

Weiss, B. (2020, July 14). Resignation letter from *The New York Times.* https://www.bariweiss.com/resignation-letter

Whorf, B. L. (1956). *Language, thought, and reality: Selected writings of Benjamin Lee Whorf* (J. B. Carroll, Ed.). MIT Press.

Zaki, J. (2019). *The war for kindness: Building empathy in a fractured world.* Crown Publishing.

Zillmann, D. (2000). Media effects: Advances in theory and research. In J. Bryant & D. Zillmann (Eds.), *Media effects: Advances in theory and research* (2nd ed., pp. 19–41). Lawrence Erlbaum Associates.

Zillmann, D. (2000). The psychology of curiosity: A review and reinterpretation. *Psychological Bulletin, 126*(5), 665–681. https://doi.org/10.1037/0033-2909.126.5.665

Zuboff, S. (2019). *The age of surveillance capitalism: The fight for a human future at the new frontier of power.* PublicAffairs.

Appendix A

Study Resources by Theme

These curated readings expand on the themes explored in each chapter. Whether you're seeking psychological depth, spiritual clarity, or cultural critique, these works provide valuable context and deeper understanding.

Chapter 1: The Nature of Offense

Theme: Emotional reactivity, ego sensitivity, and the origins of being offended.

The Righteous Mind – Jonathan Haidt. Haidt explores how our moral reactions are rooted in intuitive emotion rather than reason, helping explain why offense often bypasses logic.

The Ego Trick – Julian Baggini. Baggini investigates the illusion of a fixed self, shedding light on why personal identity feels so easily threatened.

The Untethered Soul – Michael A. Singer. Singer offers tools to observe inner reactions without attachment, helping dissolve the egoic reflex to take offense.

Chapter 2: The Need for Moral Superiority

Theme: Virtue signaling, moral posturing, and the psychology of being "right."

Virtue Signaling – Geoffrey Miller. Miller dissects how moral outrage can be used as a strategy for gaining social status rather than seeking justice.

Mistakes Were Made (But Not by Me) – Carol Tavris & Elliot Aronson. This book examines how self-justification distorts memory and morality, reinforcing a sense of superiority.

Against Empathy – Paul Bloom. Bloom argues that empathy can be a biased and performative emotion, often driven more by ego than genuine care.

Chapter 3: The Paradox of Empathy

Theme: When empathy harms, helps, or becomes self-centered.

Altruism in Humans – C. Daniel Batson. Batson presents decades of research showing that true altruism is possible—but often confused with self-serving motives.

Against Empathy – Paul Bloom. Bloom explores how unchecked empathy can lead to irrational decisions and moral blind spots.

The Compassionate Mind – Paul Gilbert. Gilbert explains how cultivating compassion activates a healthier emotional system than empathy alone.

Chapter 4: The Echo Chambers of Modern Discourse

Theme: Polarization, social media silos, and confirmation bias.

The Coddling of the American Mind – Greg Lukianoff & Jonathan Haidt. This book explores how emotional reasoning and safetyism have created a fragile discourse culture.

You're Not Listening – Kate Murphy. Murphy reveals how true listening is becoming rare—and how its absence contributes to misunderstanding and outrage.

Think Again – Adam Grant. Grant encourages intellectual humility and the willingness to revise beliefs, key to breaking out of echo chambers.

Chapter 5: The Media's Role in Outrage Culture

Theme: Sensationalism, monetized anger, and information manipulation.

Trust Me, I'm Lying – Ryan Holiday. Holiday exposes how media outrage is engineered for profit, using lies, exaggeration, and emotional hooks.

Manufacturing Consent – Edward S. Herman & Noam Chomsky. This classic work examines how media systems shape public opinion through selective coverage and framing.

Ten Arguments for Deleting Your Social Media Accounts Right Now – Jaron Lanier. Lanier outlines how social platforms exploit outrage to control behavior and keep users emotionally engaged.

Chapter 6: The Weaponization of Language

Theme: How words become tools for control, distortion, or domination.

The Symbolic Species – Terrence Deacon. Deacon explores how language shapes consciousness and social reality, with both creative and destructive potential.

The Language of Thought – Jerry Fodor. Fodor's theory delves into the cognitive structures behind language, useful for understanding how framing alters perception.

Propaganda – Edward Bernays. Bernays explains how language and imagery are deliberately used to sway opinion and manufacture public consensus.

Chapter 7: Personal Consequences of Outrage Addiction

Theme: Emotional fatigue, trauma loops, and stress-based identity.

The Body Keeps the Score – Bessel van der Kolk. Van der Kolk shows how unprocessed emotional stress embeds itself in the body, often disguised as righteous anger.

Why Zebras Don't Get Ulcers – Robert Sapolsky. Sapolsky explains how prolonged stress, including moral outrage, wears down the body and mind.

The Molecule of More – Daniel Z. Lieberman & Michael E. Long. This book explores how dopamine drives desire and outrage, creating addictive emotional cycles.

Chapter 8: Societal Consequences of Outrage Culture

Theme: Civic breakdown, eroded trust, and the loss of dialogue.

Bowling Alone – Robert Putnam. Putnam chronicles the collapse of social capital and community, showing how isolation fuels performative outrage.

The Shallows – Nicholas Carr. Carr examines how digital culture fragments attention and impairs deep thought, contributing to reactive discourse.

The War for Kindness – Jamil Zaki. Zaki offers research and hope for rebuilding empathy and trust in an increasingly divided culture.

Chapter 9: The Economics of Offense

Theme: Outrage as a business model, influence economy, and monetized grievance.

The Attention Merchants – Tim Wu. Wu traces how human attention became a commodity—and how outrage became its most valuable currency.

Surveillance Capitalism – Shoshana Zuboff. Zuboff explains how behavioral data is harvested and weaponized, shaping emotions and fueling outrage.

Ten Arguments for Deleting Your Social Media Accounts Right Now – Jaron Lanier

Lanier provides a sharp critique of how outrage is engineered to serve commercial and political ends.

Chapter 10: Emotional Resilience in a Hyper-Offended World

Theme: Self-regulation, grounded presence, and inner strength.

The Wisdom of Insecurity – Alan Watts. Watts illuminates how clinging to certainty creates suffering, while resilience is found in embracing impermanence.

Emotional Agility – Susan David. David offers tools for responding to emotions mindfully rather than reactively, essential in an age of offense.

A New Earth: Awakening to Your Life's Purpose – Eckhart Tolle. Tolle offers insight into how the ego creates division, suffering, and reactive identity, and how presence dissolves it.

Chapter 11: Reclaiming Empathy and Compassion

Theme: Reconnecting with others beyond ego and ideology.

Nonviolent Communication – Marshall Rosenberg. Rosenberg outlines a language of empathy that helps break the cycle of blame, shame, and conflict.

The War for Kindness – Jamil Zaki. Zaki combines neuroscience and storytelling to show how empathy can be trained and restored.

The Compassionate Mind – Paul Gilbert. Gilbert provides psychological strategies for building a compassionate worldview grounded in strength, not sentimentality.

Chapter 12: Cultivating Intellectual Freedom

Theme: Independent thought, inner sovereignty, and nonconformity.

Free Speech: Ten Principles for a Connected World – Timothy Garton Ash. Ash lays out a global defense of free expression as a foundational principle of intellectual freedom.

Think Again – Adam Grant. Grant encourages readers to question their assumptions and become more mentally agile in their beliefs.

How to Think – Alan Jacobs. Jacobs explores how to think deeply, generously, and independently in an age of outrage and oversimplification.

Epilogue: The Road to Emotional Sovereignty

Theme: Lasting freedom, personal integration, and conscious living.

The Untethered Soul – Michael A. Singer. Singer teaches how to let go of inner disturbances and live from a place of deep peace and clarity.

A New Earth: Awakening to Your Life's Purpose – Eckhart Tolle. Tolle helps readers transcend egoic identity and reclaim the power of present-moment awareness.

Man's Search for Meaning – Viktor Frankl. Frankl offers a timeless reminder that freedom is not the absence of struggle, but the power to choose one's response to it.

We'd Love to Hear From You!

Thank you so much for reading this book-it means the world to me. If you found it helpful, inspiring, or just enjoyable, would you take a moment to leave a review? Your feedback not only helps others but also keeps me motivated to create more valuable content for you.

Here's how you can leave a review:

1. Scan the QR code on this page to go directly to the author's page.

2. Or, visit your Amazon Orders page, find this book, and click "Write a Product Review."

**Your kind words make a big difference.
Thank you for your support!**